DECORATE
for a PARTY

DECORATE
for a PARTY

STYLISH AND
SIMPLE IDEAS
FOR MEANINGFUL
GATHERINGS

HOLLY BECKER + LESLIE SHEWRING

Jacqui
Small

First published in 2016 by
Jacqui Small LLP
74–77 White Lion Street
London N1 9PF
Text copyright © 2016 by Holly Becker
and Leslie Shewring
Design layout and photography copyright
© Jacqui Small 2016

The authors' moral rights have been
asserted.

Publisher **Jacqui Small**
Managing Editor **Emma Heyworth-Dunn**
Designer **Helen Bratby**
Editor **Sian Parkhouse**
Stylists **Holly Becker and Leslie Shewring**
Production **Maeve Healy**

ISBN: 978 1 91025 429 5
A catalogue record for this book
is available from the British Library.

2018 2017 2016
10 9 8 7 6 5 4 3 2 1
Printed in China

Q Quarto
Knows

Contents

Welcome

This book is about creating a little magic. It's about hosting joyful celebrations, showing love, sharing a good time and letting go of perfection. It's about making concrete memories in the one place where you have free rein – in your home. *Decorate For a Party* will show you how to celebrate in style without spending a lot of time or money. We're here to help you plan genuine, heartfelt occasions. We wanted to create a book detailing how we approach party planning from lighting to playlists, hostess gifts, colours and patterns, food ideas, wall décor ideas, DIY projects and hundreds of fun tips that make a party memorable. This book was born from our passion for party planning and the experiences we've had hosting parties large and small. From parties with over 100 guests in the backyard to an intimate bridal shower, we've hosted all kinds and this book is jam-packed with tips and tricks to inspire you to create your own.

Why have a party when you can reserve a table at your favorite restaurant? Well, you can do both, depending on the occasion, but remember that throwing a party allows you full control which means you can put your own creative spin on everything from music to lighting and the menu, which is extremely rewarding. Hosting at home allows you to create memories that will last a lifetime (and much more beautiful photos too!).

Think back for a moment, do you remember when you celebrated your child's first birthday around the dining room table? The smiles, the laughter, eyes aglow as a flickering cake was set before your little one? The photo booth you made, the great pictures you have of your home beautifully decorated, and how you didn't have to stress over running over time or irritating other guests – it was your home, not a public space – you could do as you pleased, and you did! This book is about making more of those moments through dinner parties, engagement parties, a whisky tasting, a baby shower for your friend… Even those crazy theme parties that end in the wee hours of the morning with everyone singing kareoke in your living room. Gatherings make a house a home. The memories you create become part of the house itself.

When it comes to decorating for a party, it's not about playing super hostess or laying out the best china or the most expensive crystal. It's more important to add character and love by considering thoughtful and fun ways to make guests feel important and cherished. When we attend flashy and expensive parties that took a lot of time and money to pull off, we often feel intimated and uninspired. You too? That's why in this book we won't show you how to create perfectly set tabletops or contrived environments. While some delight in creating the perfect party we don't have the time or the patience. Instead, we'll show you how to make the most of what you already have by using what's stored in your china cabinet, craft cupboard and pantry, but with a fresh, creative twist. You'll see hundreds of stylish yet quick and easy ways to create a beautiful party that looks like you put much more effort into it than you actually did (we like that!). Our desire is to make you feel excited about hosting parties by taking off some of the pressure. So planning can be fun, and once the party starts you can relax and really be present and enjoy your own soirée.

A party is a wonderful chance to share and gather, eat and enjoy, show your creativity (which makes you feel great and inspires guests) and to have a wonderful time filled with love, laughter, friendship and great memories. Everyone loves a good party and *Decorate For a Party* will help you to throw some of your best ones yet! So take your notebook and pen and start putting together some ideas as you flip through these pages, and most of all, have fun and pick and choose ideas from all of our chapters to craft your own unique event.

Happy celebrating!

Holly & Leslie

FIRST THOUGHTS

We find with our party planning that having a jumping-off point, a cohesive element to an event that ties food to décor and occasion, is important. It makes planning so much easier if you can visualize your celebration early on.

CHOOSING A THEME

WHILE THEME PARTIES (FOR EXAMPLE, CARTOON CHARACTERS) AREN'T OUR FOCUS, YOU CAN TAKE ANY OF OUR IDEAS AND MIX IT INTO ANY THEME, OR CREATE YOUR OWN THEME. WE'RE JUST HERE TO PLANT LOTS OF SEEDS AND YOU CAN REINTERPRET HOWEVER YOU PLEASE. MIX AND MATCH, FROM IDEAS TO COLOURS, AND ALLOW YOUR CREATIVITY TO SOAR!

Aren't themes so obvious though?

Sure, if you overdo them. A wine tasting with grape clusters on napkins, as a centrepiece and on chair cushions – yeah, you've crossed the line into tackyville and you need to pull back, a lot. But if you're hosting a wine and chocolate party, then you can discreetly weave in your theme while still keeping it classy and marrying together the various elements of the occasion, like palette, menu, drink, music, etc. (See pages 90–101 as an example of this)

Can't I just buy party supplies, blow up balloons and be done with it?

Yes, you can, we do it sometimes. We aren't telling you to get a potter's wheel and make the plates or to stitch your guests' names into the napkins. Our goal isn't to encourage perfect (yawn!) party planning, but we do want to encourage mixing in things that are personal to create warmth and add a little magic to the event. Personal and heartfelt sharing is the goal. It's better to have less decoration if it means what you do have was made by you or embellished by your hand. Skip the placemats, chargers and tablecloth and take a little extra time to tie flowers around each napkin or lay lengths of ribbon down the centre of the table to create a focal point and runner.

SETTING THE SCENE

HAVING A PARTY IS AN OPPORTUNITY TO SHARE YOUR PERSONAL STYLE WITH YOUR GUESTS. WHETHER YOU ARE HOSTING A SMALL INTIMATE DINNER OR A LARGE EVENT, TAKE THE TIME TO DECORATE YOUR PARTY. YOU CAN DECIDE HOW MUCH TIME YOU HAVE TO DEVOTE. MAYBE IT IS JUST AN HOUR TO SET YOUR DINING TABLE BEAUTIFULLY AND MAKE SOME NAPKIN RINGS, OR POSSIBLY YOU HAVE MORE TIME TO MAKE A WALL HANGING OR SOME BANNERS TO TRANSFORM YOUR ROOM. WE SUGGEST CUSTOMIZING READY-MADE DECORATING INGREDIENTS, TOO, SO THAT YOU CAN ADD YOUR STYLE IN A BEAUTIFUL, FUN AND MORE EFFICIENT WAY. WITH SOME COLOURED TAPES, PAINT, GLUE AND RIBBONS YOU CAN TURN GENERIC PARTY SUPPLIES INTO YOUR OWN PERSONAL DECORATIONS.

● Add simple stickers to lots of the same-coloured balloons to let guests know it is time to party.

● Glue a colourful paper fringe along the edge of an inexpensive white tablecloth to dress up a buffet table.

● Handwrite with a craft pen on plain glass votives to create a twinkling mantel.

● Add a little paint to some paper lanterns and hang them together in a bunch to construct a focal point to the room.

● Wrap basic plastic party cutlery with beautiful pieces of fabric.

TYPES OF PARTY

If you're hosting a party, large or small, you'll need to set some plans in place in advance. Everyone has their own special way of planning soirées, so we won't be bossy or overwhelm you. Instead, we're going to walk you through the options with some tips that have helped us with our parties. In all honesty, you can plan right down to the smallest detail, but if you aren't relaxed and don't enjoy the celebration there is little point in planning a party in the first place, right? So here are some tips to give you some zen before you begin.

THROWING A PARTY AT A HIRED LOCATION

SOMETIMES THE OCCASION CALLS FOR A LARGER CROWD, WHICH YOU CANNOT COMFORTABLY ENTERTAIN AT HOME. IN THAT CASE LOOK AROUND FOR A GOOD LOCAL VENUE.

● Decide on the size of your guest list and then you can check the capacity of a location.

● What equipment and furniture is available? Will you need to rent tables, tablecloths, napkins, chairs and stereo equipment? Can you bring in your own music?

● Is there an on-site kitchen for you to use for prep? Does your venue require that you use specific catering companies?

● What kinds of decorations are allowed in the venue? Can you tape or pin to the wall? Can anything be hung from the ceiling? Are real candles allowed or only battery-operated ones?

HOSTING STRESS-FREE DINNER PARTIES

THERE IS SOMETHING REALLY WONDERFUL ABOUT HAVING FRIENDS OVER FOR DINNER. IT CAN BE A MORE INTIMATE, RELAXED AND FUN CHANGE FROM MEETING AT A RESTAURANT. OF COURSE YOU CAN ALWAYS HAVE FRIENDS OVER FOR A TAKEAWAY AND A BOTTLE OF WINE, AS THOSE IMPROMPTU EVENINGS CAN BE THE PERFECT WAY TO STAY CONNECTED. HOWEVER, WITH SOME SIMPLE PLANNING YOU CAN PREPARE A DINNER PARTY THAT IS SPECIAL AND NOT TOO STRESSFUL.

● A nice dinner party size is around 8 to 10. Plan your guest list around people's interests and those who you think will get along well. Make sure to enquire about any food allergies.

● Plan your menu ahead of time and keep it simple. Pick a great main dish you know how to cook well, and then build out a couple of side dishes that complement your special main dish.

● You want dishes that are not too labour intensive so that you aren't cooking while guests are there. Aim for easier dishes that only take a few minutes to finish off once your guests have arrived.

● Set out an appetizer or platter just before guests arrive so that they can have something to nibble on with their drinks while you finish cooking.

A BUFFET-STYLE PARTY

THIS IS A MORE CASUAL APPROACH TO A
SIT-DOWN DINNER AND WORKS WELL WITH
SOME FORWARD PLANNING.

● Pick a general food theme and build a menu for
your buffet around it. This way all your dishes will
work well together.

● The buffet should look like it is filled with plenty
of food, so choose your table set-up wisely. There is
nothing worse than a few small dishes scattered on
a long table! Your menu can be simple but you want
to create a feeling of abundance, so that guests feel
welcome and comfortable.

● Arrange your table to create the best flow for
people getting the food. It works best if you can
access the table on both sides.

● Consider adding some height and texture on the
buffet table with cake stands, a tablecloth or runner,
and some taller decorations in the centre or at the
back where they won't be knocked over.

● You can lay out food in the kitchen on the
countertops, so guests can roam around to mingle
and snack. This encourages flow so guests aren't all
packed together in one room or around one table.

THROWING A PARTY IN A SMALL SPACE

IF YOU DON'T HAVE A LARGE LOFT OR A
SPRAWLING HOME, YOU STILL HAVE OPTIONS TO
THROW A LOVELY GATHERING, SO DON'T LET
SPACE CONSTRAINTS HOLD YOU BACK. IF YOU
LOVE TO COOK, OR EAT, OR BOTH – AND YOU
DELIGHT IN THE COMPANY OF YOUR FRIENDS AND
FAMILY – THERE IS NO REASON NOT TO USE YOUR
HOME FOR ENTERTAINING. DROP THE QUEST FOR
PERFECTION AND INSTEAD FOCUS ON MAKING
THE PARTY PERSONAL AND MEANINGFUL.

● Pull in chairs from every room to create a dining
area – you don't have to have a formal dining room
with matchy-matchy seating. Benches, stools, ladder
backs, armchairs… mix and match is in and no one
cares as long as it's comfortable.

● Turn your living room into a dining room by
draping a tablecloth on your coffee table, adding
some large lounge pillows on the floor and sharing
a relaxed meal together. Or you could borrow a
wallpaper table from a friend and set it up with
chairs, or place a few card tables together to
create a dining table. A pretty tablecloth covers a
multitude of sins!

● Skip formal sit-down gatherings to avoid over-
crowding and opt for buffet-style serving, or a
cocktail party with snacks in bowls scattered around
your home – place some near the hallway, on a
console and bar cart, others on the coffee and side
tables or on the bookshelves.

● Don't overdo your styling. Small spaces are best
kept simple when it comes to floral arrangements,
table settings, over-the-table bunting and other
decorative touches. The secret is to edit and minimize
the amount of serving trays, plates and utensils that
you use, too.

CREATING ATMOSPHERE

The most important thing to achieve with a party is that your guests relax, have fun and enjoy the event. There are things you can do to help set the mood.

WELCOMING YOUR GUESTS

● Have the table set and ready, decorations hung and everything organized beforehand. A frazzled and stressed host can set the wrong tone for the entire evening.

● Walk through the house to make sure everything is in place and you didn't leave miscellaneous things out while decorating, such as scissors and tape. Light your candles 10 minutes before the first guests are due to arrive.

● Smile and make it your mission to have fun!

LIGHTING

● Create ambiance with lighting that feels cosy and inviting, not harsh and unwelcoming. Also, candlelight always makes your home and your guests look better!

● We love candlelight, twinkle lights and dimmer switches. Just go easy on scented candles. Lots of people have allergies, they compete with perfume and aftershave, and scented candles around food is a definite no go.

● Tapers can easily tip over, especially in cramped spaces, so opt for tealights and glass votives.

THE MUSIC

● Nothing breaks party jitters like classic tunes or something mellow and inspiring. Music creates distraction – so get that playlist ready and put it on 20 minutes before the first guest is due to arrive to get you in the mood

FLOWERS

● Buy your flowers the day before with your groceries so that they have a chance to fully open and you have time to arrange them nicely. If buds are closed, force them to open by placing in very warm water.

● If you plan to have some simple unscented flowers on the table, make sure they are low arrangements, so they don't block sight lines and hinder free-flowing conversation.

Now let's explore how to bring together the elements to create magical accessories with meaning and joy. We've designed 10 themes to get you started. Let's begin . . .

CREATING WARM AND PERSONAL GATHERINGS,
WHERE FRIENDSHIP AND FOOD ARE THE FOCUS

Gather + make

THIS WARM AND CREATIVE CRAFT PARTY HAS A TOUCH OF 'HYGGE'. IN DANISH, THE WORD CONVEYS A SPIRIT OF UNCONDITIONAL LOVE AND ACCEPTANCE EXPERIENCED IN A COSY GATHERING OF FAMILY AND GOOD FRIENDS. IT SUGGESTS CAMARADERIE, AFFECTIONATE TEAMWORK, SO A PARTY THAT FEELS VERY HYGGE ISN'T PRETENTIOUS OR FORMAL. THE FOCUS ISN'T ON FEASTING, BUT BEING CREATIVE AND THINKING OF WHAT YOU CAN GIVE TO OTHERS TO MAKE THEM FEEL THE HYGGE SPIRIT, TOO.

WHAT INSPIRED US... our many Danish friends and their generous and often magical style of welcoming and entertaining guests; a stack of Marimekko plates plucked from a favourite shop; winter trips to Copenhagen and Stockholm; generic and affordable materials for crafting, since limitation usually breeds creativity; a cut-out Moorish pattern on a blanket resembling snowflakes purchased during our Marrakesh adventure together (it became our table covering); and a recycle bin for light bulbs stumbled upon at a local pharmacy that gave us immediate inspiration (and free supplies!) to create Christmas tree baubles.

SEASON
ANYTIME IS GOOD FOR
CRAFTING, BUT OUR FOCUS
HERE IS CHRISTMAS

PARTY SUGGESTIONS
CRAFTING WITH THE GIRLS,
MOTHER'S DAY (JUST SWITCH
UP THE CRAFT PROJECTS),
KID'S BIRTHDAY (AGAIN,
MODIFY CRAFTS) AND EASTER
CRAFT PARTY (COLOUR EGGS,
DECORATE COOKIES, ETC.)

COLOURS
BLACK AND WHITE WITH
METALLIC SILVER, COPPER AND
SOME GOLD

PATTERNS
GEOMETRICS, MODERN FLORALS,
PAISLEYS, STARS, DOTS AND
SOME MOORISH MOTIFS

ELEMENTS
CUPCAKE CASES
GIFT WRAP
CHINESE FOOD BOXES
PAPER STARS AND LANTERNS
WHITE GLASS MARKER
CUSTOMIZED WOODEN CUTLERY
WHITE BEADS
RECYCLED LIGHT BULBS
PAPER STRAW GIFT BAGS
CHRISTMAS CRACKERS
BIRCH WOOD LIGHT

PLAYLIST
CARLY RAE JEPSEN 'LAST
   CHRISTMAS'
JUSTIN BIEBER 'MISTLETOE',
FRANCESCA BATTISTELLI 'GO TELL IT
ON THE MOUNTAIN'
SHE & HIM 'ROCKIN' AROUND
   THE CHRISTMAS TREE'
ALAN JACKSON 'LET IT BE
   CHRISTMAS'
DIANA KRALL 'THE CHRISTMAS
   SONG'
BLAKE SHELTON (FEAT. MICHAEL
BUBLE) 'HOME'
WHAM 'LAST CHRISTMAS'

SET THE MOOD

You don't need to live in Copenhagen to create winter charm
at home during the holidays. We kept our palette modern
in black and white and mixed in a little fresh pine (a lovely
scent!), plenty of handmade and personalized elements and
the glow of warm candlelight for a welcoming, cosy mood.

OUR SCANDI CRAFT PARTY is a lovely way to pull together your friends and craft together. You can deepen friendships by making things together, whether for trimming your tree, decorating your table or creating pretty gift boxes, tags and bags. Light the candles, place snacks at the end of the table in creative containers, play your favourite tunes and celebrate the season!

OREOS ON A STICK

Slide a lollipop stick into an Oreo cookie, and drizzle melted chocolate over it until it's covered. Roll in sprinkles, and stick in a styrofoam block to dry. Then add a masking tape flag to the stem for a pretty and easy food idea.

CHINESE TAKEAWAY

Cardboard food boxes are easy to find in craft shops, so stock up for picnics and parties. You can decorate them with stickers, tape and markers. We've used black masking tape to create a Swiss cross, a pattern found everywhere in Scandinavian design.

CUSTOMIZED CUPS

Spruce up paper cups with a hole puncher in a flower shape combined with patterned paper and a glue stick. Disposable wooden spoons were hit with a bit of black matte spray paint the night before (on the handle only).

MODERN CRACKERS

Place three round chocolates in crepe paper, seal on each end with gold tape in a classic cracker shape and wrap a black-and-white stripe paper band around them for a little pattern.

ADDING WARMTH

With black and white, things can easily feel cold. Warm up the scheme with candles, texture and some pine on the tabletop. We've used a thin white blanket from Morocco as a tablecloth to add texture and some understated pattern that mimics snowflakes.

6 ways:
STAMP NAPKINS

1. We used sticky-backed foam sheets from the craft store for our stamps. Simply cut out your desired shape, then peel back the covering and stick it to another piece of foam that is slightly larger than your stamp shape. We started with a triangle in a random pattern.

2. This is a quick design to execute. Use a small square cut from the foam sheet and repeat.

1

2

3

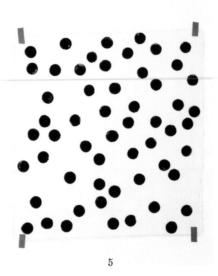

4

3. A soft matte fabric paint is used to create these designs as the paint washes nicely and has a softer feel. Be careful not to use the harder dimensional fabric paints. A star is cut from the foam and repeated. We used a square edged paintbrush to touch up in a few places.

4. Ceate this fun linear design by placing four foam strips together on one stamp.

5. For this design we've used a round sponge stamp from the craft store.

6. We created two stamps and each had two different triangle foam shapes. Don't be afraid to touch up your design with a small square-edged paintbrush to sharpen some of the edges of the design if necessary.

5

6

TWINKLE LITTLE STAR

Create star ornaments for your tree, branches or to tie to a gift. You can string beads onto copper wire (we used 58), then snip the wire at the end, leaving enough to twist and shape into a loop for hanging. Shape into a star and add a small piece of black-and-white striped ribbon to finish.

ADVENT BRANCH White boxes and bags are stamped with numbers, filled with little advent treats, then hung on this beautiful branch with white and black twine. Hang securely on the wall with nails and some fine wire wrapped around each end of the branch.

HOW TO ORGANIZE A CRAFT PARTY

1. Decide on what you will make together. Will you wrap gifts? Make ornaments? Work on a group project together? Sketch out your ideas.

2. Decide how many 'make it' stations you'll need to set up. If you are just working on one project, like wrapping presents, you can put all of the supplies in the middle of the table.

3. If you're working on individual projects, decide what each project will look like (more or less) and make an example. This is not only to display on the table so guests have a blueprint to work from, but also so you'll know which supplies you'll need to purchase in advance.

4. If you want an organized approach, place supplies in glassine bags labelled by project, so supplies needed to make a beaded star ornament, for instance, are in a single bag. Then, when guests arrive, they can each quickly grab a kit to work on.

5. If you have very creative friends, you can count on them to completely change up the projects, so you can take a more freestyle approach. Ask guests to make whatever comes to mind using the supplies on hand. You still can

have a few examples on the table to kick-start the ideas. If you have alcohol and good music at your party, expect creativity to soar (wink!).

6. Purchase extra supplies in case extra guests arrive, or mistakes are made, and guests need to make their project a second or third time.

7. It's okay to tell friends to bring a bag of goodies from their own craft closet that they'd like to share. You can reserve an empty bowl or two for guests to dump their loot into, and mix it all together for the group to use.

8. If you are having a gift wrap party, make sure you remind your guests to bring their gifts with them to wrap, too!

9. Serve snacks that are uncomplicated and aren't greasy or give guests grubby hands. Keep food on a separate table. Have a signature drink or two and place away from the crafting area.

10. Take a group shot at the end, asking guests to hold up the project they've made that they love most – this will be a fun photo to share online or just to keep and enjoy for years to come.

Make something for the wall that your guests want to try at home, too.

Top chairs with fur throws to cosy up the room.

Cut papers into shapes of trees and glue onto plain gift boxes.

Wrap a birch branch with twinkle lights to create a warm glow.

STRAWS ON PAPER BAGS

Paper straws are not just for drinks. These gift bags show another way to use them. First cut to size and glue white cardstock to a paper bag. Trim a few straws to create a tree motif and adhere with a glue stick. Top the tree with a button. Fill with your gift and tissue paper. Easy but lovely!

CUPCAKE CASE TREE

Make this mini tree using white mini cake cases, double-sided tape to secure to the wall, and for the star, black-and-white washi tape.

to make: Start with the top case and secure to the wall. Tape a dark string below the case and let it drop straight down to use as a guide to keep your rows straight as you work. Create rows of 1, 2, 4, 6, 8 and 10 cases and finish the bottom of with a row of 3 to form the base. Cut 4 equal-length strips of washi tape and create a cross, then overlap with an X. That's it!

COOL CONTAINERS

Use cupcake liners, Chinese takeaway boxes and mini muffin forms as bowls for craft items like markers, tapes, beads, glitter and sequins to keep everything in its place while crafting.

note: On the next page we'll break down how to make these light bulb ornaments, you'll love them!

WINDOW DISPLAY

Using generic shop-bought party supplies, group similar colours and hang them at different heights from textural ribbons.

LIGHT BULB ORNAMENTS

Recycle light bulbs by turning them into
ornaments for your tree. Some you may
choose to spray paint (we used matte
black on some of ours) and others you
may opt to keep as is, especially
if they are frosted. Use a glue stick and
apply sequins, glitter or beads. Allow
to dry overnight and then twist copper
wire around the base several times
and create a loop for hanging.

CREATIVE WRAP IDEAS

White butcher paper, gold washi tape, white twine and a hand-cut gold paper feather.

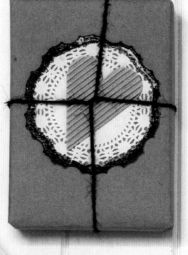

Kraft paper, paint-dipped doily, corrugated kraft paper heart, finished with black twine.

White butcher paper, black glitter tape with gingham ribbon.

Handmade bamboo skewer star finished with washi tape and tied on with black twine.

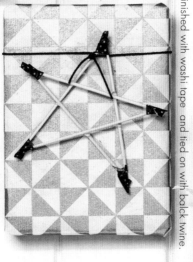

White butcher paper with polka dot scrapbook paper, white office tag, black ric-rac ribbon and a flagged paper clip.

White-paint-splattered kraft paper wrap, lacy ribbon and a white paper snowflake.

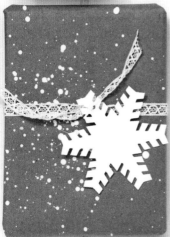

Merry Merry ♥

Black-paper-topped box, white twine with kraft star.

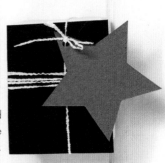

White butcher paper, black cardboard ornament wrapped with white yarn and tied on with black twine.

PAPER-FRINGE TREE

THIS SUPER-EASY, INEXPENSIVE TREE IS PERFECT FOR SMALL SPACES
OR TO DECORATE A TABLETOP IN YOUR HOME. IT IS MODERN AND MINIMAL
AND LOOKS LOVELY WITH WHITE TWINKLE LIGHTS AND SOME CANDLES
NEAR BY. YOU CAN PURCHASE LARGER SHEETS OF CARDBOARD AT
MOST ART SUPPLY STORES.

YOU WILL NEED
hot glue gun, cardboard,
black paper, lightweight
white paper, black tape,
scissors, craft knife

STEP ONE Cut the
cardboard to your
desired triangular tree shape.

STEP TWO Start about
5cm/2 inches from the
bottom of the tree and cut
approximately a 5cm/2 inch-
wide strip of white paper to
a length just wider than the
width of the tree.

STEP THREE Glue the top
edge of the strip of white paper
to the cardboard and then trim
the width to the angle of the
cardboard.

STEP FOUR Create a fringe
along the bottom edge of the
white strip of paper you just
glued down. Make the cuts
about 1cm/½ inch apart.

STEP FIVE Repeat with
more white strips, making sure
to overlap each one over the
previous one.

STEP SIX Finish by adding
a black strip of paper to cover
the exposed 5cm/2 inches of
cardboard along the bottom
of the triangle. Use black tape
to wrap around the sides of this
base, or just wrap the black
paper around.

New + romantic

THIS SOFT, TACTILE LOOK IS A WARM MIX OF ORGANIC MATERIALS AND TEXTURES,
HANDMADE DETAILS AND A TOUCH OF VINTAGE GLASS. IT IS RELAXED AND FEMININE,
PERFECT FOR A PARTY WITH GIRLFRIENDS. NAPKINS WERE DIP DYED FOR THE TABLE AND A
WALL HANGING ASSEMBLED WITH EUCALYPTUS, STRING AND A PAINTED BRANCH. DELICATE
GARDEN ROSES ARE A BEAUTIFUL CONTRAST TO RUSTIC WOODEN TABLES.

WHAT INSPIRED US... chalky bleached colours; the smell of eucalyptus in Golden Gate
Park; long conversations while drinking rosé; handwritten notes; summer gatherings; roses in
porcelain vessels; driftwood from the beach; natural fibres, creamy-toned Heath ceramics; and
realizing that creating a wonderful evening for a special person is worth the effort.

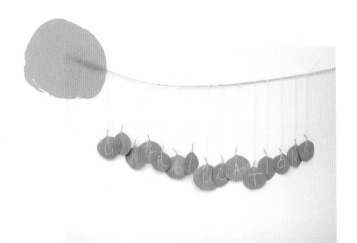

SEASON
SUMMER
OR EARLY AUTUMN

PARTY SUGGESTIONS
BRIDAL SHOWER,
SIGNIFICANT BIRTHDAY,
DINNER WITH GIRLFRIENDS

COLOURS
CHALKY MINT, DENIM
BLUE, PEACH, SAND,
WHITE, BLEACHED
WARM GREY, WHEAT

PATTERNS
SHIBORI DESIGNS
AND SIMPLE MEXICAN
WOVEN PATTERNS

ELEMENTS
EUCALYPTUS
HAND-DYED COTTON
LEATHER TWINE
VINTAGE GLASSES
NATURAL STRING
WOOL
BRANCHES
DRIFTWOOD
HANDMADE PORCELAIN VASES
GARDEN ROSES
HANDWRITING ON GLASS

PLAYLIST
MAX FROST 'LET ME DOWN EASY'
VACATIONER 'PARADISE WAITING'
MATT SIMONS 'CATCH &
    RELEASE' (DEEPEND REMIX)
BROODS 'MOTHER & FATHER'
GLASS ANIMALS 'GOOEY'
NORA EN PURE 'COME WITH ME'
RYN WEAVER 'STAY LOW'
MONTGOMERY 'PINATA'
PACIFIC AIR 'FLOAT'

SPECIAL GUEST

We dedicated a specific chair for the guest of honour at this bridal shower to sit on to open her gifts, a perfect focus for a photo opportunity. For dining, you can create a relaxed atmosphere by setting an assortment of cushions around low tables – a wonderful alternative to a formal setting. Guests really enjoy lounging in this way.

This soft, romantic theme works beautifully for this CASUAL BRIDAL SHOWER, and would also be lovely for a summer birthday party or an all-girls evening to celebrate friendship. All our details are thoughtfully done to give some warm, homemade, feminine charm. Many can be made ahead of time and set aside for the day of the party.

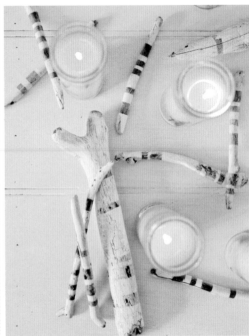

GIFT WRAPS

'Furoshiki' is the Japanese term for the fabric-wrapped gifts we made for our guests. We added a sprig of wheat with the natural cotton.

PIE GARLAND

Decorate a pie to sit out on a dessert table with a few sprigs of non-toxic flowers that can easily be removed before cutting and serving.

NATURAL STIRRERS

Even hot drinks can have a pretty drink stirrer! These bamboo drink stirrers are embellished with a tiny sprig of eucalyptus.

SOFT STRIPES

We painted driftwood sticks, masking off stripes first with tape in various widths. Once the paint dried we took off the tape to reveal the natural wood.

CALLIGRAPHY CANDLES

Basic jar candles are made special thanks to
Canadian artist Kate Campbell's calligraphy,
done with a black 'for glass' pen. Our idea
here was to have words that represent positive
wishes or intentions. Each guest lights a candle
and gives the wish to the guest of honour.

SIMPLE DIY
OJO DE DIOS

A HALLWAY CAN HAVE A FRESH NEW LOOK FOR ANY PARTY WITH THIS UPDATED CRAFT PROJECT. THE OJO DE DIOS, ALSO KNOWN AS GOD'S EYE, HAS TRADITIONALLY BEEN MADE AS AN ACT OF CELEBRATION OR BLESSING FOR A HOME. WE THOUGHT IT WOULD BE BEAUTIFUL TO MAKE THEM USING NATURAL WOOL IN COLOURS THAT COMPLEMENT THE DECORATING THEME. THEY LOOK GORGEOUS AS A GROUP OF THREE.

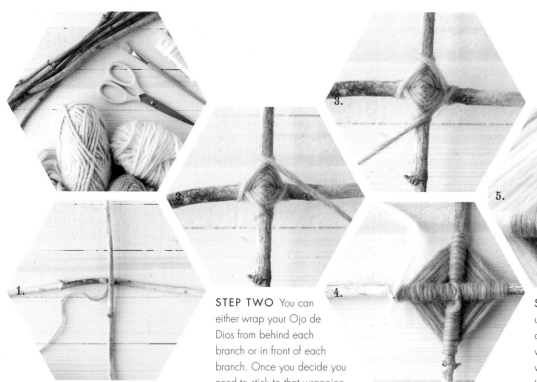

YOU WILL NEED branches cut down to a similar length, assorted wool, scissors, paintbrush, white craft paint, thin wire.

STEP ONE If you like, paint the branches with some white craft paint. Place two branches of relatively similar thickness and length together in a cross position. Secure with wool crosswise as shown.

STEP TWO You can either wrap your Ojo de Dios from behind each branch or in front of each branch. Once you decide you need to stick to that wrapping approach. In this case we went to the first branch from the front, wrapped around the branch and then on to the next one.

STEP THREE Move on to the next branch in a clockwise sequence. Make sure to wrap around the front, then around the branch and onto the next branch. Cross over from the front and then around to the back and around and on to the next.

STEP FOUR It is nice to use a few differnt colours. To change colours tie on your new wool when you have your wool wrapping around the back so that the knot does not show on the front of your design.

STEP FIVE Once you have finished wrapping your wools, create a secure way to hang your Ojo de Dios by attaching a thin wire around the cross of the two branches at the back. This way your project will hang flat on the wall.

EUCALYPTUS WALL HANGING

This eucalyptus and branch wall hanging was
created easily on the day of the party. We simply tied
eucalyptus sprigs to both ends of 20 pieces of fine
white string cut to various lengths, and then hung them
over a sprayed white branch. Fine wire wrapped
around each end of the branch created loops for
hanging the piece up exactly where we wanted it.

WRAPPED SUCCULENTS

We wanted guests to take home these potted succulents as a party favour to commemorate the occasion. We made a little wrap with white paper and then finished it off with a creamy white string.

NATURAL HEART

Branches picked up from the local flower shop were bent to create a heart, secured at each end with some natural twine. We then added a few sprigs of baby's breath and eucalyptus.

6 ways: NAPKIN RINGS

1. Using a piece of string 15cm/ 6 inches long, thread on wooden beads. Tie the ends of the string together to create a circle. You could paint one of the beads an accent colour – we chose white for this look.

2. Using a thick strand of wool we created a natural napkin ring with an added sprig of eucalyptus. We think this would also look nice with sage or rosemary!

3. Securely tie two strands of thick natural rope together that are approximately 15cm/6 inches long. Then braid the two pieces together and finish by fastening with string to the other beginning end to create a circle. You will need to overlap them slightly to tie together. You may want to adjust the length of your rope pieces depending on the size of your napkins.

4. Simply tie a strand of leather around your napkins to create an informal napkin ring. We wanted to wrap it a few times so we used a long piece and then just tied with a simple knot instead of a bow.

5. Using the cardboard roll from a finished paper towel roll, cut to the desired width (about 5cm/2 inches). Fix the end of some thick cotton twine with hot glue to the inside of the roll, then wrap from inside to outside around the roll till it is covered. Fix the other end with another dab of glue. Decorate with a fresh or fabric flower.

6. Using the same technique as before, cover a cardboard roll with thin natural twine. Using a small piece of the same twine, attach a fresh leaf with a simple knot to the ring.

DRINKS TAGS

Handwritten tags are fastened with
string to the stem of the glasses so that
they can easily be identified.

Fresh + modern

ALWAYS RELAXED AND COOL, WITH ITS CLEAN LINES AND GRAPHIC SHAPES THIS LOOK WOULDN'T BE RIGHT WITHOUT A LITTLE BIT OF GLAMOUR OR A TINY HINT OF DRAMA. YOU CAN EASILY BRING THIS FLAIR TO A SIMPLE DINNER PARTY WITH SOME TROPICAL FOLIAGE, METALLIC GOLD DETAILS AND A GRAPHIC PRINT.

WHAT INSPIRED US... Palm Springs; Mid-Century Modern furniture; bold prints; deep green foliage; and, of course, some shiny metal accessories. We both have a soft spot for Los Angeles and wanted to find ways to bring some of that LA vibe into a party at home. With this story you will find some fun projects to quickly glam up basic party essentials such as white napkins and glass candle holders.

SEASON
SUMMER OR EARLY AUTUMN
OR WINTER

PARTY SUGGESTIONS
COCKTAIL PARTY
NEW YEAR'S
OSCAR AWARDS NIGHT
BIRTHDAY

COLOURS
BLACK, WHITE, GREEN,
WOOD BROWNS, GOLD,
ORANGE AND A LITTLE PEACH

PATTERNS
BOLD GEOMETRICS,
SIMPLE FOLIAGE

ELEMENTS
AIR PLANTS
SUCCULENTS
WOODEN CHOPPING BOARDS
TEAK ACCESSORIES
MONSTERA LEAVES
SHINY GOLDS
GLASS CYLINDERS
MATTE BLACK
MARBLE
TROPICAL FLOWERS

PLAYLIST
MOBY 'PORCELAIN'
DISCLOSURE (FEAT. SAM SMITH) 'LATCH'
THE ANTLERS 'FRENCH EXIT'
THE TEMPER TRAP 'SWEET DISPOSITION'
EL PERRO DEL MAR 'CHANGE OF HEART'
MR LITTLE JEANS 'RESCUE SONG'
   (RAC REMIX)
TOUCH SENSITIVE 'PIZZA GUY'

A bold palette provides that hint of drama for a SUMMER DINNER PARTY FOR FRIENDS, with bright fuchsia, matte black, shiny gold and a mix of greens. From outside on the patio to inside the dining room we wanted to keep the colours consistent. A help-yourself drinks set-up and little dishes set out before dinner on the table for guests to pick at helps the relaxed mood.

GREEN GARNISHES

Make it easy on yourself and serve one standard cocktail for the evening. Guests can then personalize their drink with a variety of garnishes you provide.

FOIL BUNTING

We wanted a bunting that was grown-up, not crafty, so we made a simple one by folding over small pieces of gold metallic paper, then glued them onto gold twine.

MODERN TABLETOP

When you have a beautiful tabletop you don't need to protect, like this shiny black marble, lay your spread sans tablecloth. It's a modern way to serve and it feels less formal.

BALLOON STICKERS

Black balloons are decorated with a few gold stickers picked up from the office supply store.

NATURAL PLACECARDS

Use a gold pen on greenery to customize your place settings.

SPECIMEN CHART

A science-class-style wall hanging was assembled with a couple of black-painted dowels and a piece of heavyweight paper. Drawing pins were pressed into each side of the top dowel to attach the cord for hanging. We glued on some monstera leaves with a little dab of hot glue so that they could be removed and we could use this hanging again.

LEAF PHOTO WRAP

Make your own wrapping paper by taking a photo of a single leaf or a few leaves on a white background and then printing it out. This works well for smaller gifts. If you want to wrap large gifts you can use an online printing company to print out larger sheets or rolls of wrapping paper from your own photographs.

CYLINDERS AND LEAVES

Cylinder vases are used with only one leave placed in water. The look is simple and very pretty. Of course, the water must be kept crystal clear.

FRESH WELCOME

Just a few leaves in an assortment of vases can brighten up the hallway and greet guests arriving for the gathering.

SIMPLE DIY
GOLD-PAINTED HURRICANES

THIS DIY IS QUICK AND EASY, TURNING REGULAR OLD GLASS HURRICANE VASES INTO
STUNNING CANDLE HOLDERS FOR YOUR PARTY. THEY LOOK BEST WHEN GROUPED
TOGETHER, AND THE POSSIBILITIES FOR THE PATTERNS ARE ENDLESS! USE THEM AS A
PRETTY ARRANGEMENT IN THE CENTRE OF YOUR DINING TABLE OR GROUP THEM ON
A NEARBY BUFFET, SIDE TABLE OR MANTELPIECE.

1.

3.

5.

YOU WILL NEED
washi tape, paintbrush,
gold glass pen, gold acrylic
paint, plain glass candle
holder and candle

4.

2.

STEP FIVE Create a
few more complementary
patterns on various sizes of
glass holders. These are for
decorative purposes only and
are not water safe.

STEP THREE Carefully
remove all the tape.

STEP FOUR Use a gold
pen if needed to touch up the
pattern edges.

STEP ONE Determine your
design and then use tape to
create your masked-off pattern
on the glass.

STEP TWO Paint the areas
of your pattern on the exposed
glass. Let dry completely and
then do a second and even
third coat depending on the
intensity of colour you desire.

6 ways:
NAME CARDS

1. Add a few brushes of gold craft paint to your printed-out names. Then use a small wooden craft cube that has been dressed up with sparkly gold tape to keep your name card in place. It acts like a mini paperweight!

2. Create a stamp out of foam sheets from the craft store. Print out your guest names on a piece of paper, randomly stamp the sheet, then cut it up to create similar-sized cards. .

1

2

3. Print out the names on white paper and then use plain wooden craft blocks that have been painted with white acrylic craft paint to create simple modern geometric shapes. As long as you don't glue these blocks on you can use them again!

4. A metal tube found in packs in the jewellery-making section of craft stores is used to add a modern touch to this camellia sprig. Add a dab of hot glue to the end of the branch before putting on the tube so that the tube stays securely in place.

3

4

5. A plastic gem is spray painted with a matte gold spray paint and then glued to a simple card with your guest's name. You can find these plastic gems in the craft store.

6. Create a simple folded name card on white paper. Spray paint paper straws gold to resemble a metal tube. Cut the painted straw to the length of the card and secure with a few dabs of hot glue to the bottom edge of the card. Clean, modern looking and fast!

5

6

BAR CART BASICS

STUMPED ON HOW TO LAY OUT A BASIC BAR CART? DON'T BE. HERE'S A CHECKLIST TO MAKE IT A BREEZE.

1. Bar cart or small table
2. Recipe book
3. Bottle opener
4. Drink stirrers
5. Glasses – tall and short. You can also stock wine and champagne glasses, but you could drink wine from short glasses so you don't have to weigh down your cart with too many different glass types.
6. Ice bucket and serving tongs
7. Shaker
8. Tonic water and assorted sodas and mixers
9. Favourite booze
10. Bowl of lemons and limes
11. Cutting board, small knife
12. Pretty straws
13. Cocktail napkins
14. A small bouquet of flowers, a stem of something green, like a palm leaf or a protea flower.

Pure + simple

A QUIET CELEBRATION OF NATURAL BOUNTY, SIMPLE ROMANCE IS MINDFUL OF THE SEASONS WITH ITS EMPHASIS ON FRUITS AND FLOWERS AS DECORATION. MIX-MATCHED PLATES COLLECTED FROM CHARITY SHOPS OVER THE YEARS SIT ALONGSIDE VINTAGE CUTLERY AND NATURAL LINENS. INFUSED WATERS LOOK DECORATIVE AND BEAUTIFUL ON THE COUNTER FOR GUESTS TO HELP THEMSELVES. THIS LOOK IS PERFECT FOR THANKSGIVING OR OTHER HARVEST DINNERS THAT GIVE THANKS FOR THE PRODUCE OF YOUR VEGETABLE GARDEN OR EVEN THE LOCAL FARMERS' MARKET!

WHAT INSPIRED US… raw linen aprons; rolls of brown kraft paper; the colour of crunchy pears; light caramel-coloured wood; beautiful handwriting in ink pen; pressed cranberry juice; delicate illustrations on vintage tableware; strings of little globe lights twinkling after dark; and yearning for another special dinner that lingers for hours with friends and loved ones.

SEASON
AUTUMN, LATE SUMMER

PARTY SUGGESTIONS
THANKSGIVING,
HARVEST DINNER, BIRTHDAY

COLOURS
GREEN, CREAM, VIOLET, YELLOW

PATTERNS
DELICATE VINTAGE MOTIFS

ELEMENTS
VINTAGE CHINA
BERRIES
KRAFT PAPER
LINEN
AUTUMN FRUITS
'NAKED'-SIDED CAKE
RUSTIC POTTERY
ROSEMARY SPRIGS
INFUSED WATER
VINTAGE SILVERWARE
HOMEMADE PRESERVES

PLAYLIST
RAY LAMONTAGNE & THE PARIAH
DOGS 'FOR THE SUMMER'
ANGUS & JULIA STONE 'BIG JET PLANE'
GARY JULES 'WICHITA'
RUSTED ROOT 'SEND ME ON MY WAY'
BON IVER 'PERTH'
IRON & WINE 'NAKED AS WE COME'
BEN HOWARD 'OLD PINE'
ALEXI MURDOCH 'ALL MY DAYS'
BOY & BEAR 'FALL AT YOUR FEET'
BAHAMAS 'LOST IN THE LIGHT'
LISA HANNIGAN 'LILLE'

THIS ELEGANT DINNER PARTY FOR SIX combines natural elements and thoughtful details. This event is not at all fussy and feels a little nostalgic for a life that is simpler and more peaceful. Fresh garnishes were made ahead for the drinks and special homemade preserves are placed at each setting for guests to take home after the meal.

NATURAL linen placemats are laid over a pure white tablecloth. The subtle colour change between the two fabrics is calm and inviting.

HOMEMADE cranberry syrup is used to create a light and refreshing drink. Blueberries on a bamboo skewer and a sprig of rosemary are used to garnish.

BOTTLES and vases grouped together on the table create a relaxed yet thoughtful look.

VINTAGE mismatched silverware collected over the years looks charming.

FRESH BERRIES

A simple sponge cake picked up from the bakery is finished off with some whipped cream and then topped with mixed berries, a few non-toxic flowers and a sprinkling of icing sugar.

INFUSED WATERS

Infused waters are delicious, easy to prepare and are healthy alternatives to sugary beverages. Have fun experimenting with different fresh fruits and herbs such as mint or coriander. Cinnamon sticks and vanilla beans are also lovely and provide subtle flavouring.

HANDWRITTEN

A menu can become a beautiful wall hanging
for your gathering. Kraft paper is wrapped
around a bare branch at each end and then
glued into place. A few sprigs of fresh greenery
are glued along the top and then the menu is
hung from some twine that is tied on securely at
each end of the top branch.

CLOTHESLINE

Cotton string was tacked on
the wall and then little sprigs
of leaves, flowers, berries
and pods were hung from
it by miniature clothespegs.
This fresh wall hanging is
inexpensive, and easy to put
up to decorate plain walls in
your dining area.

6 ways:
PLACE SETTINGS

1. Lace trim was snipped to mark a place setting and simply laid on top of the tablecloth. A linen napkin is topped with a round cocktail napkin with sprigs of greens on top and a strip of paper with 'Let Us Eat' stamped on with dark brown ink. Small baking tins become tealight holders. Sprigs and blooms are scattered on the table to bring in colour and a touch of nature. A menu card is tucked beneath the napkin, with pattern peeking through that complements the subdued palette of the tabletop.

2. A plate holds some candles wrapped in greens – we just used wire and sprigs and made these simply by hand-forming little circles and placing candles in the middle.

Ribbons dance down the centre of the table with petals from a daisy. A larger wreath was placed on a plate – in the centre a small candle has a tag that says 'Make a wish' (created on the computer, printed out and trimmed with scissors) pinned onto ribbon. Silverware was placed in a napkin tired with string.

3. Metal baking tins mimic the floral shape of the soup bowl. A pretty votive candle greets each guest with hello on a strip of paper (or write your guests' first names) – just punch a little hole in the top of the paper, pull the wick through, bend beneath the candle and tape in place. A simple dahlia head continues the petal-shape theme. The linen runner in blush rose adds additional colour.

1

2

3

4

5

6

4. Mixing linens makes a table feel warm and natural. A napkin placed below a gorgeous handmade plate topped with tied silverware against nubby linen is simple but elegant. Use your computer and a favourite font to create a 'Thankful for' slip, placed near the dinner plate with a wooden pencil. This is such a wonderful way to connect people at a dinner. We've done this before and asked each guest to share their list during the evening and it always made the gathering more magical and intimate. A small sprig of green in a tiny vase is as simple as you can get but beautiful still. We used a paper bag from the grocery store and a circle punch to add some polka dots to the table. A wine glass is topped with a strip of lace trim and the name of the guest is placed on top. Small candles in tin holders work nicely with the colour of the napkin and patina of the vintage silverware.

5. Add a wreath to just one of your place settings for the birthday girl, bride-to-be or someone who is being honoured at a special gathering. You can even ask her to wear it in her hair or hang it later from the back of her chair, and definitely invite her to take it home. Use two runners on your table, placed along each side to use as placemats. A darker linen napkin in an eggplant tone adds contrast. Simple twine looped around silverware is easy but pretty. A tiny note on a small plate is a personal touch.

6. A little scroll can be for your menu or a sweet note to your guest. We found these adorable candle holders, which are also vases, and it was love at first sight! We mixed in some greenery and used the same greens to form a little wreath and tied on the guest name. A tiny bottle with sprigs of flowers acts as a sweet takeaway hostess gift.

SIMPLE DIY
WOVEN TRIVET

A COFFEE OR TEA GATHERING IS GIVEN A LITTLE EXTRA HANDMADE TOUCH WITH A SIMPLE WOVEN TRIVET. THIS PROJECT IS A WONDERFUL WAY TO USE UP LITTLE LEFTOVER SCRAPS OF YOUR FAVOURITE FABRICS.

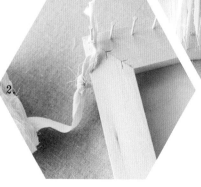

YOU WILL NEED a frame of some kind in the desired size – (we used one that was 25cm x 25cm/10 x 10 inches), scrap fabric strips, nails, hammer.

STEP ONE Hammer in your nails along two facing sides of your frame. We used 14 nails along each side of this frame.

STEP TWO Tie on your fabric securely around the first nail on one side.

STEP THREE Cross your fabric to the opposite nail on the other side, wrap around and then head back across to the next nail. Wrap all the way across in this way.

STEP FOUR When you reach the final nail on the opposite far corner from where you started tie your fabric to the nail and then trim off the end.

STEP FIVE You are now ready to weave in the opposite direction with your fabric. We decided to use some colour for the woven fabric. Tie on your fabric to a corner nail and then weave your fabric over the first strand and then under the next strand, moving across the frame. When you reach the end, turn your board around and work your way back across, moving over and under, over and under.

STEP SIX Once you have woven your entire trivet, take it off the frame and then flip over your woven piece and securely knot your loose end piece around one of the other crossing pieces of fabric. You can trim off any excess fabric once you have made your knot.

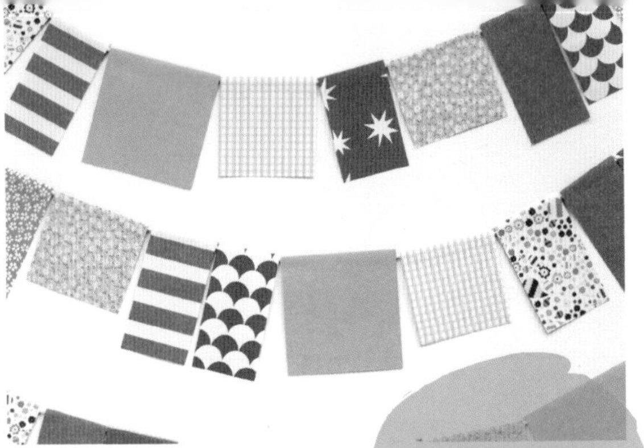

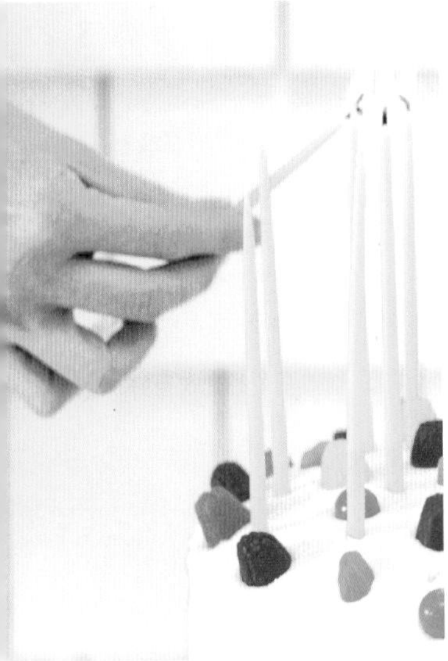

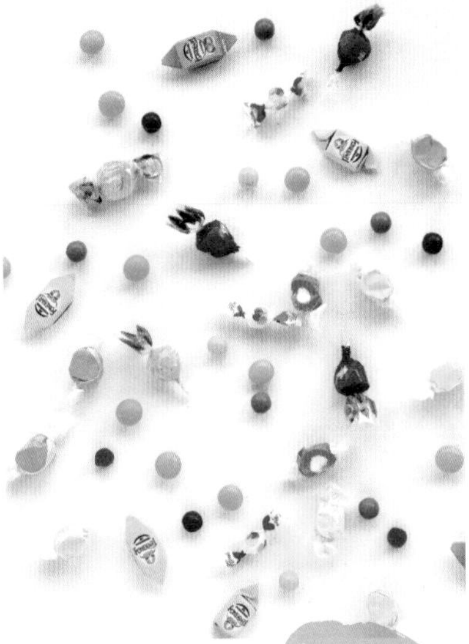

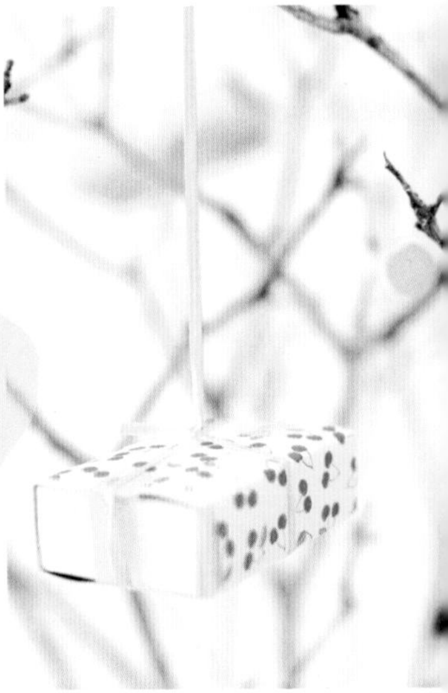

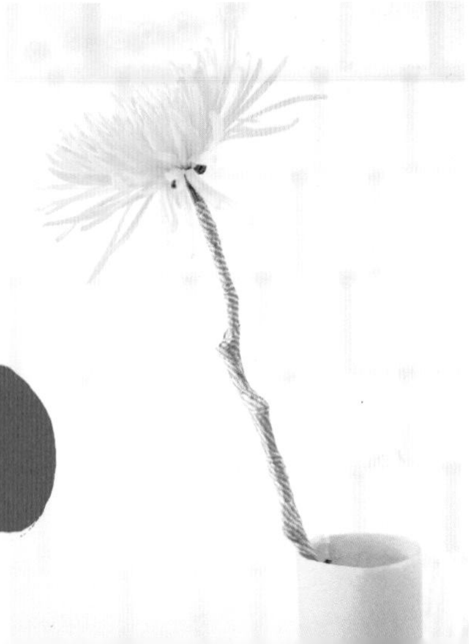

A sweet treat for you

Happy + bright

POPS OF COLOUR BURST ALL OVER A PRIMARILY WHITE SPACE IN THIS FUN PARTY LOOK. TISSUE PAPER FANS ARE CUSTOMIZED WITH STREAMERS AND CREPE PAPER, AND SWEET TREATS ABOUND. IT'S TIME TO CHILL THE BUBBLY, BUST OUT THE COLOURFUL CONFETTI AND ORDER IN LUNCH TO CELEBRATE A WONDERFUL PERSON ON THEIR BIRTHDAY.

WHAT INSPIRED US... a bold palette of primary colours mixed with mint and peach; bright dishes stacked on clean white shelves; thick crepe paper to wrap around vases and cake stands; swimming-pool blue honeycomb tissue fans; sweet shops with candy in every colour; tying cutlery with patterned ribbons and fabric scraps; drink stirrers that make a glass of orange soda spectacular!

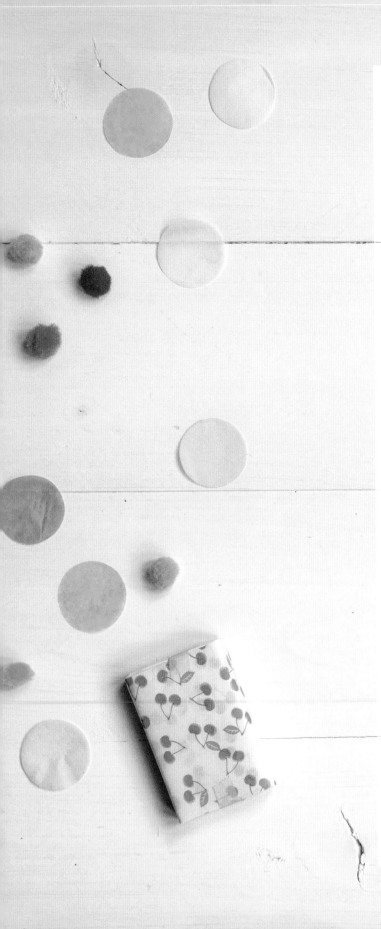

SEASON
SPRING, SUMMER OR WINTER

PARTY SUGGESTIONS
BIRTHDAY
GRADUATION
BABY SHOWER
CELEBRATION BRUNCH

COLOURS
RED, CITRUS YELLOW, DENIM BLUE, MINT,
PEACH, WHITE, A TOUCH OF AQUA

PATTERNS
SWEET FLORALS, GINGHAM, POLKA DOTS
AND SIMPLE GRAPHICS

ELEMENTS
WASHI TAPE
SKINNY TAPER CANDLES
TISSUE PAPER FANS
GLASSINE BAGS
PAPER CONES
COLOURFUL POM-POMS
PAPER AND FELT CONFETTI
PLASTIC CANDY APPLE RED CUTLERY
TAPE AND RIBBON GARLAND
CREPE PAPER
CANDY TUBES

PLAYLIST
CARLY RAE JEPSEN 'RUN AWAY
   WITH ME'
INGRID MICHAELSON 'THE WAY I AM'
FEIST '1234'
TAYLOR SWIFT 'STYLE'
HAIM 'FALLING'
KEHLANI (FEAT. COUCHERON) 'ALIVE'
HAILEE STEINFELD 'LOVE MYSELF'
ELLIE GOULDING 'ANYTHING
   COULD HAPPEN'
ROBYN 'CALL YOUR GIRLFRIEND'

This is such a happy and playful party to celebrate the SPECIAL BIRTHDAY OF A GIRLFRIEND WHO IS STILL A KID AT HEART! We truly enjoyed putting together this party because it is about whimsical details and creating a warm sense of nostalgia for those dreamy childhood parties that we loved so much and remember so intensely.

PATTERN PLAY

Use a charger and washi tape under your plate to make an interesting placemat. Elevate plastic party cutlery with some pretty fabric scraps – it keeps them together and looks pretty.

DRINKS FLAG

Fabric tape on the end of lollipop sticks become instant drink decorations. Lollipop or candy sticks can be found at most craft stores in the sweet-making section.

INSTANT POLKA DOTS

Make a quick stencil and use some craft paint to paint a pattern on your own tablecloth or table runner. We used paper here for the runner as it is a super inexpensive way to instantly make your table look brighter. Felt confetti is sprinkled on the table to add different colours and a different scale of polka dot.

TREAT BAG

Use glassine bags to hold sweets and fold over and finish with a little pom-pom added with glue

GIFT TREE

A gift tree is made from a few branches decorated with a little white paint and pom-poms. Tie on small favour boxes that your guests can carry home.

Little matchboxes from the craft store are wrapped with bright patterned papers and then filled with a few sweets and some sparkly sequins.

GUESSING JAR

Use a pretty jar filled with candy on the table to
have a guessing game. Whoever comes closest to
guessing the number of sweets wins a prize. Fun
for birthdays or showers, this could be filled with
colourful treats to match any party scheme.

PAPER DECORATIONS

Simple bunting on the wall is made from
tape and a ribbon. You can embellish paper
wheels with streamers and crepe paper.

VASE WRAPS

Cover odd bottles with a simple crepe paper wrap fixed with stickers to make your flower containers match your party theme. Wrap the stems with tape to add some pattern.

SWEETIE TUBES

Fill these plastic tubes from a party supply shop with candies all in one of your party colours to make a graphic little gift for guests to take home.

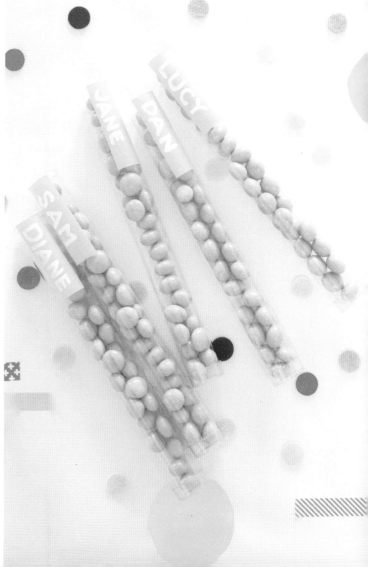

TAKE THE CAKE

Why not decorate your cake
stand? Here we tiered one cake
stand on top of another and
decorated the edges with crepe
paper. Bright candies and candles
all one colour can take a simple
white cake and make it 'party'
ready. Super colourful and cute.

CANDY CONES

Use sturdy paper to form a large cone and staple shut and glue at the seam. Once dry, decorate with washi tape, confetti, ribbon as trims, pom-poms, glitter or anything else that makes you smile. Use a paper punch to create a hole on each side about 1cm/½ inch from top. Thread through ribbon and knot the ends inside the cone. Hang from drawing pins or nails (make sure they are strong) and add sweet treats. We've used fruit-flavoured German marshmallows.

CHEERS STATION

A simple bar area can be created with some cardboard letters and craft paint. Use balloons filled with water and than freeze to create a colourful ice bucket.

6 ways:
DRINK STIRRERS

1. Using a mint sprig as a skewer, thread berries on the mint stem. This is a great way to use up mint that is growing too tall in your herb pot or garden.

2. Using a 20cm/8-inch lollipop stick or a bamboo skewer, tie on a ribbon with a tight knot to secure in place. Simple and a great way to add a little colour!

1

2

3

4

3. Create a paper flag as shown and then use a white pen to write 'Cheers' on it. Attach with a dab of glue to a 20cm/8-inch lollipop stick.

4. Using a food-safe bamboo skewer, thread edible fruit onto the skewer. We started with a grape so that the balled melons would not slip down the skewer. This is a fun edible stirrer!

5. Using a food-safe bamboo skewer or a longer lollipop stick (found in many craft or cooking stores) thread on coloured beads, securing the first one with a dab of glue. Finish the top with a glued-on paper heart. Make sure to keep coloured beads above the line of the glass, as they are there for decoration only!

6. Using a 20cm/8-inch lollipop stick or a bamboo skewer, carefully attach a bubble gum ball to the end of the skewer. We found it easier to make a small hole in the ball first and then wiggle it on the end of the stick.

5

6

CHEERFUL CHANDELIER

YOU'LL LOVE MAKING THIS QUICK AND EASY CHANDELIER TO SPICE UP YOUR BRIGHT AND CHEERFUL SOIRÉE. IT'S AFFORDABLE, TOO. IN FACT, YOU MAY WANT TO MAKE A FEW TO HANG ABOVE A LONG TABLE – THREE TOGETHER LOOK GREAT, SPACED EVENLY. OR MAKE ONE AND HANG A DISCO BALL IN THE CENTRE FOR A LITTLE SPARKLE AND TO MIMIC A LARGE LIGHT BULB.

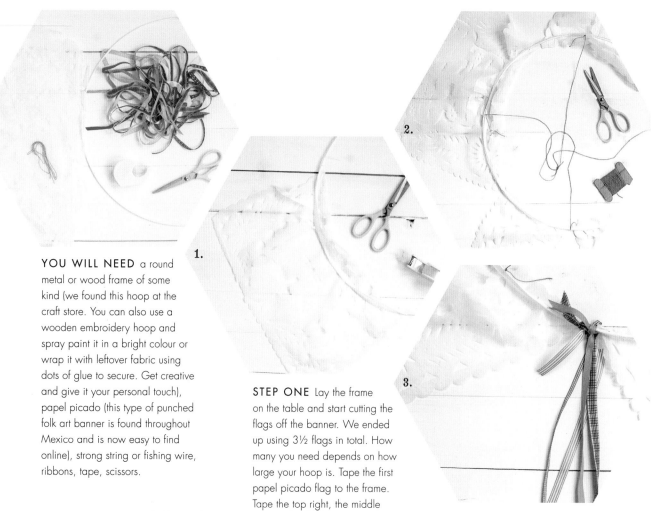

YOU WILL NEED a round metal or wood frame of some kind (we found this hoop at the craft store. You can also use a wooden embroidery hoop and spray paint it in a bright colour or wrap it with leftover fabric using dots of glue to secure. Get creative and give it your personal touch), papel picado (this type of punched folk art banner is found throughout Mexico and is now easy to find online), strong string or fishing wire, ribbons, tape, scissors.

STEP ONE Lay the frame on the table and start cutting the flags off the banner. We ended up using 3½ flags in total. How many you need depends on how large your hoop is. Tape the first papel picado flag to the frame. Tape the top right, the middle and the left. Make sure the flag is sitting evenly on the frame so it's not wavy or uneven.

STEP TWO Continue with the next flag, and the next, until the hoop has all of the flags in place. Next, use strong string to create a big 'X' and tie it to the frame. This will be what you use to hang from a hook in the ceiling.

STEP THREE Tie ribbons from the hoop in the gaps where each flag meets the next. Once the hoop is hanging in place you can stand back to see if you like the results or if more ribbon is needed.

note: Make sure to balance the amount of ribbon you use at each point or else the chandelier will start to tilt.

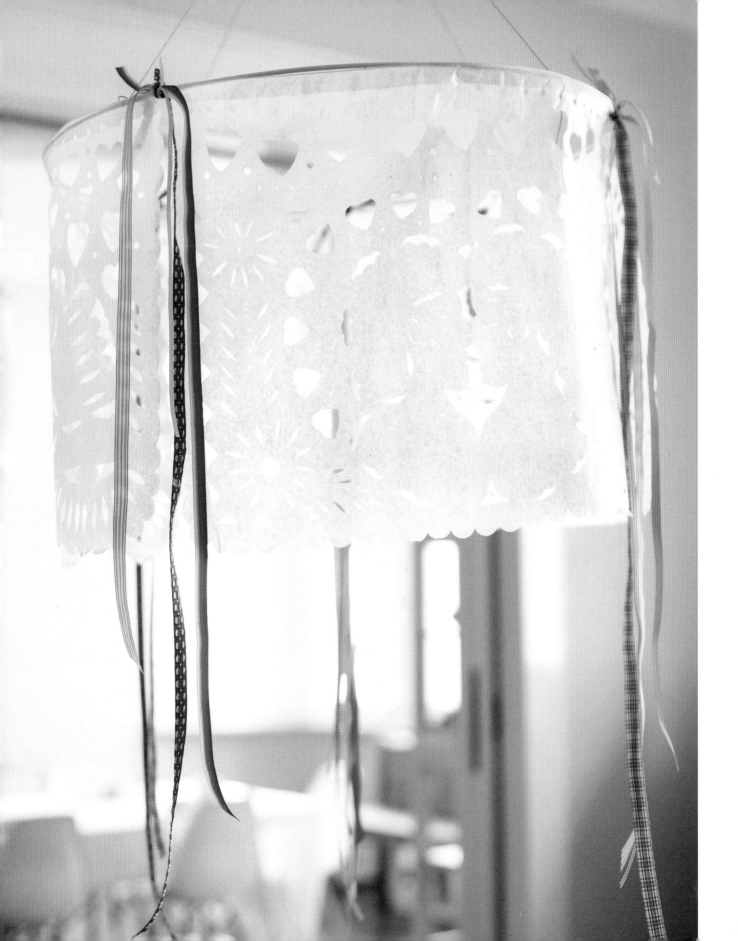

Warm + cosy

COSY, INVITING, SMOOTH, THIS STYLE SAYS COME STAY AWHILE...SMALL-SCALE FLORALS
PAIR WITH GEOMETRICS, AND VELVET RIBBONS, COPPER WIRE AND CONCRETE CANDLE
HOLDERS UNEXPECTEDLY COMPLEMENT ONE ANOTHER. RICH AND LUSH SEASONAL PICKS
FROM THE LOCAL FLOWER SHOP ADD TEXTURE AND A TOUCH OF THE OUTDOORS. THIS LOOK
IS PERFECT FOR A WINE AND CHOCOLATE PARTY, WHISKY TASTING, HOUSE-WARMING PARTY
OR A MEAL PLANNED TO WELCOME THE HARVEST.

WHAT INSPIRED US... Florentine papers from the art store; dusty finds and muted colours from
trips to vintage shops; country house interiors; autumn weather; dark cherry-toned dahlias combined
with velvety dusty miller (senecio) spotted at a local florist; our love for chocolate and fine wine; a
set of matte black silverware; wondering what we could do with all of our leftover paper straws
from previous parties (see our DIY); and a favourite ribbon shop we both love in Germany.

SEASON
AUTUMN

PARTY SUGGESTIONS
HOUSE-WARMING, WINE OR
WHISKY TASTING, ANNIVERSARY,
FATHER'S DAY, THANKSGIVING,
FAREWELL PARTY

COLOURS
PUTTY, PURPLE, BLACK, DEEP
BLUE, EMERALD GREEN, RUST,
COPPER, PALE DENIM, CREAM,
LIME, MUSHROOM, DARK
SALMON, TEAL

PATTERNS
TRADITIONAL FLORENTINE PRINTS
AND MORE MODERN ONES
WITH FLORALS, PLANTS AND
GEOMETRIC MOTIFS. FARROW
& BALL HORNBEAM WALLPAPER
FEATURING HEDGEROWS FROM
THE BRITISH COUNTRYSIDE
THAT MIMIC CLOUDS

ELEMENTS
PATTERNED PAPERS
RUSTIC WOOD
VELVET RIBBON
CHAIN LINK GARLAND
DIAMOND PENDANTS
COPPER WIRE
PAINTED GLASS VASES
WINE BOTTLES WITH BANDS
GOLD PEN
DAHLIAS
BARS OF WRAPPED CHOCOLATE
CORSAGES AND BUTTONHOLES

PLAYLIST
AMY WINEHOUSE 'ME & MR.
  JONES'
JANET JACKSON 'CAN'T B GOOD'
THE SAINT JOHNS 'OPEN WATER'
JARRYD JAMES 'THIS TIME'
MARY J BLIGE 'THERAPY'
MATT GRESHAM 'WHISKEY'
AMANDA JENSSEN 'THE END'
LANA DEL REY 'WEST COAST'

For this WINE + CHOCOLATE DINNER PARTY, held to celebrate the engagement of friends, we transformed a living area into a space to dine. If you entertain regularly, develop a system that is quick and easy to set up. Store a folding table (ours collapses and slides under the bed), drag stools in from the kitchen, add some folding chairs and you're ready to celebrate!

PATTERNED RUNNER

For the centre of the table, tape pieces of A4 /8.5 x 11 inch sheets of paper to form a runner.

PERSONAL WIRE

Using a white piece of paper, wire cutters and thin copper wire from the craft store, write the guest name in your best script and then use it as a template, laying the wire against the paper and matching it to your handwriting as you bend and twist. Each name takes less than a few minutes but guests will love it because it's unique.

BRING IN TEXTURE

Matte black cutlery is gorgeous and perfect for a moody setting like this one. Bundle and tie silverware together with velvet ribbon to add a bit of colour.

PAINTED GLASS

We painted transparent glass containers with dark petrol acrylic paint. After the party, soak vessels in the sink with warm water and washing up liquid for 5 minutes and all the paint peels off. Takes minutes, trust us! Then you have the transparent container ready to paint again for the next party.

EDIBLE PLACE CARDS

Buy your favourite chocolate bars, unwrap them and rewrap using pretty papers. Secure with velvet ribbon and create a name tag for the centre.

MAKE GUESTS FEEL SPECIAL

Give guests something to wear in their hair or pin to their shirt. These were made using flowers and mixing in some agave and feathers. Some are large and others more petite, and they definitely make guests feel special, plus it dresses up the event in case you want to take photos. If your party is a special event, like a wedding anniversary or bridal party, you can also request a dress code so everyone matches, so photos come out looking just gorgeous and so well coordinated! These mini corsages also look very lovely on a place setting, or you can arrange them on a plate on a table near the entrance so guests can select their own.

HIDE THE WINE

No, we're only kidding – keep the wine flowing for this dinner party! For fun, wrap bottles in the same patterned paper that you've used on your tabletop and for the chain bunting above the table – it's a nice way to coordinate things. But it can also be fun for guests to guess what they are drinking, and from which part of the world. Of course, the labels will come off quickly as curiosity piques, but at least the presentation upon entering the room is impressive!

RIBBON REPEAT

We love to repeat themes, so adding a velvet ribbon to the stem of a wine glass to coordinate with the ribbon used elsewhere in your room, is a nice touch.

GLASS LABELS

If you'd like to skip wine tags on glasses, buy a gold glass marker (you can remove it easily with soap and water) and write the names of one of your guests on each glass before they arrive.

6 ways:
CHAIR BACKS

1. Create small loops with paper, staple together and loop through the next paper, stapling again. Repeat until you've created a mini chain. When you get to your last link, loop through the chair and staple again.

2. Remove corks and tie vials to ribbon, then tie to chair. Add blue and copper sequins and sprigs of pretty things from the garden. No water needed.

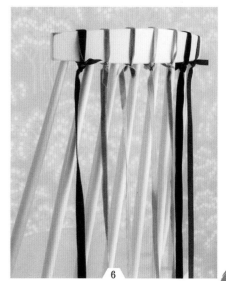

3. Tie a string of yarn to your chair back, cut and fold papers to coordinate with the tabletop, then fold over and secure in place with a glue stick. Cut the papers multiple times to create a fringe effect.

4. Tie a medium-sized honeycomb ball to your chair back and hide the typical white string they come on with multiple ribbons in your favourite colours, one over the other, to conceal the white cord.

5. String dried apple rings (available at most grocery stores) onto chunky wool yarn. Cut a rectangular strip of linen and use a black calligraphy pen (we used weight 3.5) and write your guest's name on it in your best handwriting. Fold over one edge of the strip and cut a hole through the linen, loop ribbon through and tie to the yarn.

6. Tie lengths of ribbon in moody tones from your chair back, allowing them to just touch the floor.

SIMPLE DIY
GEOMETRIC HIMMELI PENDANT

WE LOVE HOW THESE FINNISH-STYLE DECORATIONS ADD AN UNEXPECTED ELEMENT, BEING SO MODERN AND GRAPHIC. YOU CAN PAINT THEM ANY COLOUR AND ADD THEM TO ANY OF THE PARTIES WE SHARE IN THIS BOOK, THEY'RE SO VERSATILE AND FUN TO MAKE.

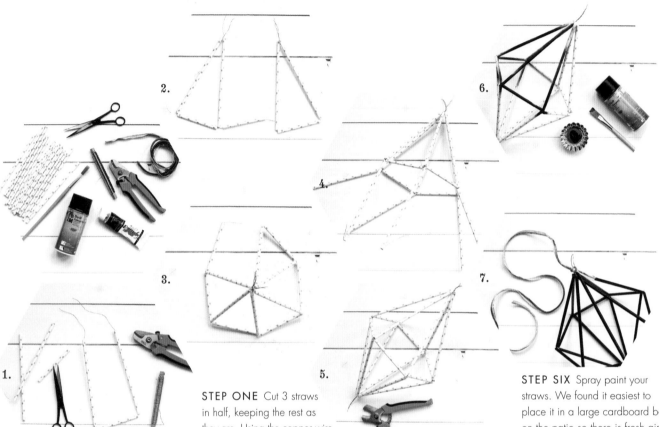

YOU WILL NEED thin copper wire, wire cutters, ribbon, 15 straws but buy a whole pack to allow for error. (if you can find solid black, definitely use them for this project as it's easier and faster! If not, you can always paint them as long as they are paper) black matte spray paint (not high gloss), black acrylic paint, paintbrush.

STEP ONE Cut 3 straws in half, keeping the rest as they are. Using the copper wire, thread through 1 regular straw, 1 short straw and 1 regular straw to form a triangle.

STEP TWO Twist the top to secure. Create 3 of these triangles. Then connect all 3 triangles by twisting the tops together.

STEP THREE Using 3 short straw, twist onto base to connect all triangles forming the top of your diamond pendant.

STEP FOUR Use 6 regular. straws and thread through a piece of copper wire, bending one end of the wire upwards to keep each straw in place. Twist and add each straw to the bottom of each triangle.

STEP FIVE When all the straws are attached, gather at the bottom and twist them together. You should have a complete pendant now.

STEP SIX Spray paint your straws. We found it easiest to place it in a large cardboard box on the patio so there is fresh air and the spray doesn't damage anything around you. Let it dry for 4–5 hours or overnight. Once dry, you will see spots you've missed. Use acrylic paint and a paintbrush to touch up and complete.

STEP SEVEN You can continue by making a few more to form a cluster as we did, or you can just hang one in your favourite spot. Add ribbon to the top by creating a loop with the leftover wire and tying the ribbon to the loop. If you want, you can also add ribbons from the bottom as streamers to make it more festive.

Simple chain made using
Florentine papers, a paper
cutter and staples.

Festive + fun

THIS IS A COLOURFUL MIXTURE OF MEXICAN-INSPIRED DECORATION THAT BURSTS WITH A FEELING OF CELEBRATION FOR A SUMMER PARTY WITH GUESTS OF ALL AGES. WE DECIDED ON A REALLY BOLD GESTURE OF COLOUR WITH BRIGHT HANDMADE PAPER FLOWERS, SET AGAINST A COOLER BACKDROP OF WHITE FOR SOME BREATHING SPACE.

WHAT INSPIRED US... sliced watermelon; blooming bougainvillea; Mexican Lotería cards; Otomi textiles; piñatas filled with sweets; dreaming of holidays to the Yucatan; simple paper crafts; a hand-painted sombrero; fruit-infused drinks; and parties where little kids and grandparents can join in the fun together.

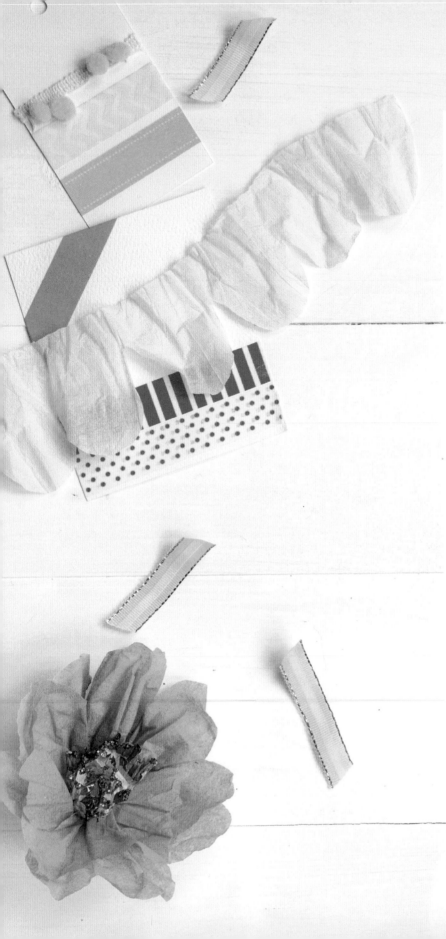

SEASON
SUMMER

PARTY SUGGESTIONS
SUMMER BARBECUE, BIRTHDAY FOR
ALL AGES, GRADUATION

COLOURS
FUCHSIA, YELLOW, ORANGE,
MELON, AQUA, PURPLE

PATTERNS
OTOMI EMBROIDERY, MEXICAN
FLORAL AND STRIPES

ELEMENTS
PAPEL PICADO BANNERS
HAND-PAINTED SOMBRERO
PUREED MELON DRINKS
PAPER FLOWERS
PINATA
POM-POM FRINGE
SILK FLOWERS
MEXICAN LOTERIA CARDS
HAND-PAINTED MARACAS
WASHI TAPE
PAPER CUTLERY PACKS

PLAYLIST
JAMES TAYLOR 'MEXICO'
ZAC BROWN BAND 'KNEE DEEP'
ALAN JACKSON 'IT'S FIVE O'CLOCK
   SOMEWHERE'
ZAC BROWN BAND 'CASTAWAY'
LOW STARS 'MEXICO'
JIMMY BUFFETT 'MARGARITAVILLE'
KENNY CHESNEY 'BEER IN MEXICO'

FLORAL FIESTA

In order to showcase all this colour it is important to balance it with some white space. This helps the splashes of colour to really pop. We decided on white papel picado banners for the ceiling and white table coverings to support all the colourful additions that surround the room.

To accommodate A LARGE FAMILY GET-TOGETHER we planned this occasion around a long buffet table that guests could access from all sides. To help with the flow and avoid crowding, the colourful fresh juice drinks were served on a different table. The whole event was given huge energy and impact with vibrant colour.

PHOTO WALL

Create a floral wall by attaching paper flowers with a glue gun to a large piece of stiff fabric or foam-core board. This bright wall is perfect for a party photo booth backdrop!

PARTY PINATA

It is easy to give a generic party-store piñata a makeover. Simply dust it with some white spray paint and add a few fabric flowers with a hot glue gun. Voila! Now this piñata is ready for a party!

BANNERS

Hang ribbons on your papel picado banners to match your colour scheme.

PICK UP A PACKET

Fold a selection of A4/12 x 8½-inch pieces of
paper to create colourful packets to keep utensils
and napkins organized on a casual buffet table.

PAPER FLOWERS

THERE ARE QUITE A FEW STEPS TO THESE PAPER FLOWERS, BUT THEY ARE WELL
WORTH THE TIME AND ONCE YOU HAVE MADE A COUPLE OF THEM THE PROCESS
BECOMES FASTER. TO MAKE SMALLER VERSIONS JUST OMIT THE INSIDE YELLOW
PIECES AND USE FEWER SHEETS, CUT SMALLER, FOR THE OUTER PETALS.

YOU WILL NEED
assorted colours of tissue
paper, fuzzy pipe cleaners,
scissors

STEP ONE Carefully stack
approximately 12 sheets of
tissue paper, lining up all the
edges carefully. We decided
to use 4 yellow for the centre,
these are stacked on top, then
2 or 3 white and then 6 sheets
of orange. Start to fold all
sheets over at the same time in
5cm/2-inch folds. Now fold
back the other way, and repeat
accordion style until you have
folded all the paper.

STEP TWO Unfold all the
paper carefully and take out the
yellow paper that will be used for
the centre of the flower. Fold the
yellow paper back in pleats, then
fold the folded paper in half. Trim
off half of the unfolded ends.

STEP THREE Make 5cm/
2-inch long cuts into the trimmed
edge of the folded yellow paper.

STEP FOUR Now fold
the white and orange
sheets back up together and
fold in half. Trim the unfolded
edges together with a rounded
edge for your petals. If you find
them too thick to trim all together
do half at a time.

STEP FIVE Carefully unfold all
your papers, place them back in
their original stacked order and
then fold back up all together.

STEP SIX Fold all the papers
in half and wrap a pipe cleaner
through the centre of the folded
tissue paper. Twist to secure.

STEP SEVEN Start with one
side of the yellow paper and
gently pull out and fluff up one
piece of the tissue. Separate
each piece as you work through
the layers of the tissue paper. Be
careful not to pull too hard on the
papers as they rip easily.

STEP EIGHT Continue on the
other side, gently separating and
pulling up each piece of tissue
paper and fluffing it until you
have a full flower shape.

SET UP A DRINKS TABLE

Wrap a round table with a few various widths of paper to make a fun inexpensive table covering. Some of the pieces were cut to make a festive fringe and others were scalloped to finish it off.

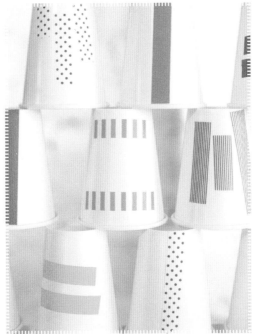

JUICE FOUNTAIN

Aguas Fresca is a delicious non-alchoholic drink made from fresh puréed fruit, in this case melon, some water and a little sugar.

COLOURFUL TAPE

Paper cups for a crowd! Why not add some bright washi tape to basic white paper cups? The look is fun and everyone will know which cup is theirs!

SWIZZLE

A little tissue paper is cut with a fringe and then wrapped around a bamboo skewer with washi tape. Add a fruit garnish to elevate these drinks in paper cups.

6 ways: GOODY BAGS

1. A brightly patterned paper is folded over the top of the bag and then two holes are punched through the paper and the bag. An orange twine is used to tie through the holes.

2. Some leftover pom-pom fringe is used in three colours to decorate the top portion of the bag. We cut each piece of fringe to the width of the bag and then applied with hot glue.

1

2

3. A piece of patterned paper is cut to the dimension of the front of the bag and then cut further into four angled pieces. Glue on the four pieces and then add a few coloured pom-poms with hot glue to the front.

4. Three fringes are made out of tissue paper and then glued onto the bag to create a three-tiered effect. We used three strips of tissue paper for each tier and made the fringe cuts before gluing onto the bag.

3

4

5. Fabric flowers from the craft store are glued with dabs of hot glue to decorate the front of the bag. For a further pop of colour we then added a few snips of yellow crepe paper.

6. Brightly coloured craft paints are used to make gestural marks on the white paper bag with a wide brush.

5

6

52

LA MACETA

19

LA GARZA

39

EL NOPAL

41

LA ROSA

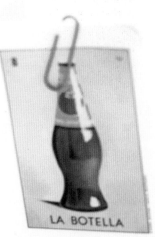

LA BOTELLA

MEXICAN 'LOTERIA' CARDS

Colourful and graphic goody bags are assembled with plain white bags, turquoise paperclips, some bright yellow washi tape and Mexican 'Lotería' cards, which can be found easily online.

Forest + family

THIS IS A GATHERING OF FRIENDS AND THEIR LITTLE ONES BENEATH A CANOPY OF TREES TO CELEBRATE THE PLEASURE OF EXPLORATION AND THE BOUNTY AND GENEROSITY OF NATURE. THIS GATHERING IS A PORTABLE PARTY THAT CAN BE PACKED USING ONLY A FEW LARGE BAGS. CHILDREN CAN EASILY ENTERTAIN THEMSELVES FOR HOURS IF GIVEN A SPOT TO EXPLORE AND THE TOOLS TO DO IT, WHICH ALSO MAKES THIS A FAMILY-FRIENDLY AFTERNOON.

WHAT INSPIRED US...torn fabrics; a rustic traditional German beer garden table; a favourite wool blanket; simple brown takeaway boxes; colourful floral fabrics sourced from a shop with a lovely owner who always cuts more than you've ordered without adding a penny to the price; specimen kits that we enjoyed as children recreated in a simple way to encourage exploration for our younger guests; the weather and mood of late summer/early autumn weather with its changing leaves and crisp air; teepees; the challenge of creating something special and memorable out of very little; and keeping the overall look inexpensive and relatively simple to prep.

SEASON
LATE SUMMER/EARLY AUTUMN

PARTY SUGGESTIONS
GARDEN PARTY
CHILD'S BIRTHDAY PARTY
FAMILY REUNION

COLOURS
BROWN, FRESH GREEN, CREAM,
RASPBERRY, BLACKBERRY, ORANGE,
BURNT UMBER, DARK YELLOW

PATTERNS
PLAID, SMALL-SCALE FLORALS,
NATURE MOTIFS

ELEMENTS
TORN FABRIC BUNTING
BROWN PAPER PACKAGING
DECORATIVE JUICE BOTTLES
PAINTED CUTLERY
MAPS
SPECIMEN KITS
TEEPEE
HANDMADE SIGNS
PINE CONE PLACE SETTINGS

PLAYLIST
ALLMAN BROWN 'SONS AND
   DAUGHTERS'
LAURA VEIRS 'NIGHTINGALE'
AMY SEELEY 'WALK TO THE PARK'
BIRDY '1901'
JAMES MORRISON 'BEAUTIFUL LIFE'
DAVID POE 'TAFFETA'
ED SHEERAN 'PHOTOGRAPH'
PASSENGER 'LET HER GO'
JOHN MAYER 'HALF OF MY HEART'

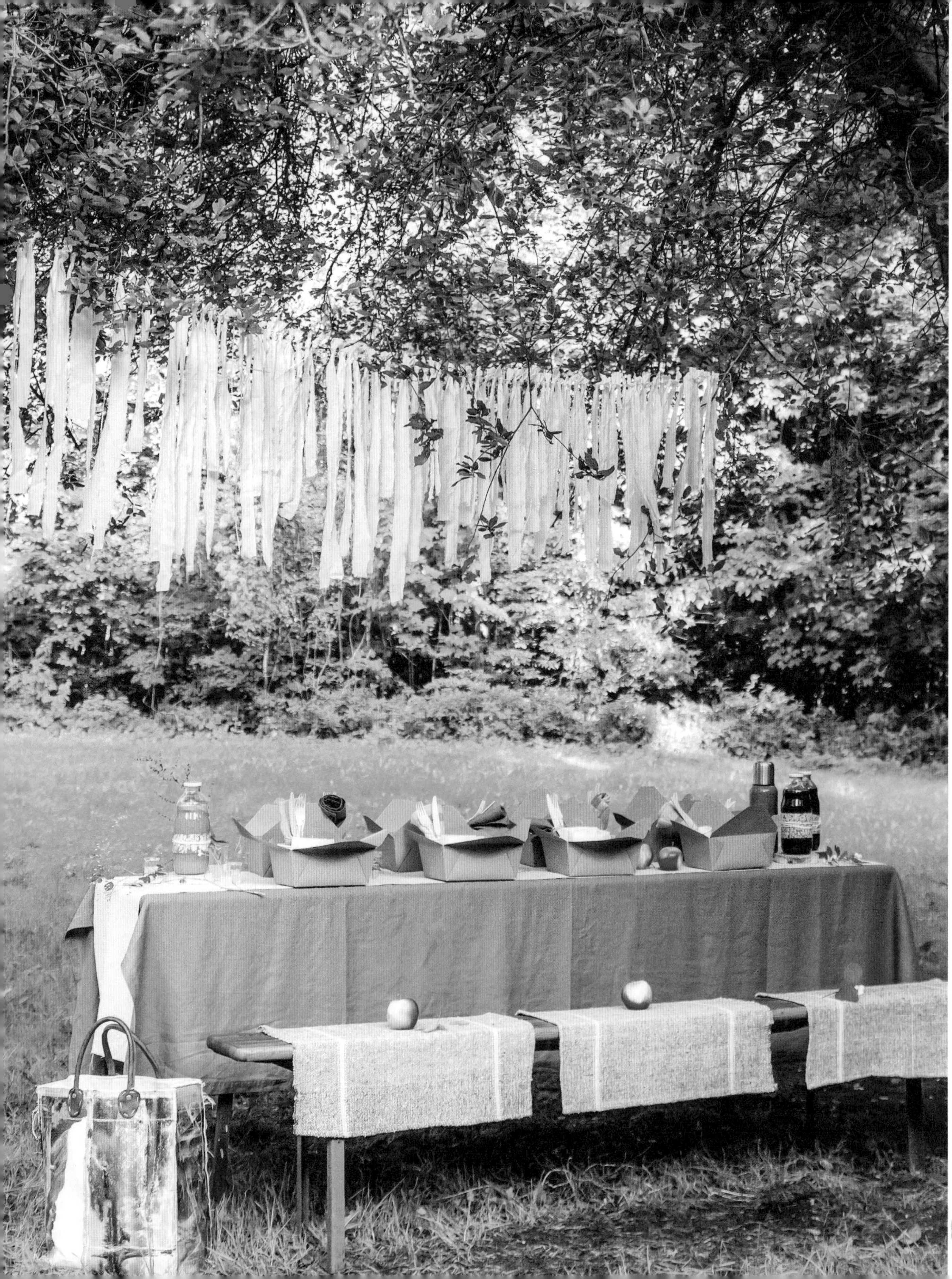

Our FOREST PARTY is perfect for parents of young children who love to explore nature. Whether you live near a forest or park and have access to public picnic tables, or the party is for a special occasion and you want to venture further and pack a folding table and benches in your car, an outing in the autumn as temperatures start to cool is an idea your friends will love.

KRAFTY LUNCH

We packed lunch in kraft paper takeaway boxes. To personalize, each was tied with torn fabric strips and presented with a sprig of something green from the forest.

FOREST CAKE

A cake is dressed up in a forest theme with mini animals, sprigs of rosemary to create little trees and bunting created using two kebab skewers, string and some strips of washi tape. This is easy to assemble – just bring your supplies and add once you arrive.

FINISHING TOUCHES

Wooden cutlery was given special, albeit simple, custom treatment by painting the tips with white acrylic paint. Leave to dry overnight and tie to a cloth napkin with string.

FRUITY TREATS

Glass fruit-juice bottles can be customized easily (skip plastic, they don't look as nice). Pour out a little of the juice to make space. Cut up fruits that complement the juice and add to the bottle. Cover the labels with fabric bands using a glue stick and some string. Apply a kraft sticker on the lid to identify the juice.

SCAVENGER HUNT

Print out favourite photos and tape to a tree as something pretty to behold. But there's more...after you've eaten, invite guests to take a photo and they will find a scavenger hunt listed on the back – a fallen branch, flower, pine cone, fern, moss, an empty snail shell, etc. The number of items to find shouldn't be overwhelming and it's more fun when children join in. The first person to find the most from their list wins a prize.

MARK THE SPOT

Make a simple marker to direct guests to the picnic site. This is a branch wrapped with string, faux fur and linen. We used a wooden knife as our arrow and stamped PICNIC on it so friends could easily locate us.

PERSONAL PINE CONES

Set up a welcome table for your gathering
– it doesn't need to be complicated. Lightly
spritz pine cones with white spray paint and
allow to dry overnight. Name tags written in
gold pen add a personal touch and allows
guests to pick and mark their own seat.

PERSONALIZED PRETZELS

Line a wooden fruit crate with a large fabric napkin
and tuck away some lovely fresh pretzels from the local
bakery. Use fabric scraps to add tags with guests'
names on them – use a hole punch to slip the fabric
through. You can write a personal message on the
other side of your tags specific to each guest.

CHILDREN'S SPACE

Construct a teepee using found branches and pine. You can google scouting websites before you set off so you know how to make it secure.

LITTLE EXPLORERS

Children love parties outdoors so try to include them! The secret is to have plenty of fun things for them to do, so they entertain themselves while parents relax. Our specimen kits (in brown bags) include a plastic magnifying glass, notebook, a pencil, insect images and stickers, a roll of washi tape, some gummy snakes and an apple.

CREATE MINI BOOKS

Encourage kids to tape their forest finds into their little books and label them. Parents can help so the project can be fun and educational for all.

SHOW THE WAY

Wrap maps in brown kraft paper and tie with handmade tags so little guests can use them to explore the area with their specimen kits. Place them on a tray decorated with fresh picked non-poisonous mushrooms and pine – simple but beautiful.

MAKE IT COSY

Bring extra throws and sheepskins to add warmth for guests (old and young!) who prefer to sit on the forest floor instead of at the table.

6 ways:
FOOD TO GO

1. Pack a lovely forest picnic in this handled berry basket. We love how the holes on the sides look like a face! Wrap the plastic handle with white grosgrain ribbon, add ribbons to the sides, neatly fold a large napkin around the meal you've prepared and secure with a piece of masking tape or a sticker. Top with fresh greenery or a flower.

2. Kraft paper food trays are easy to find and two combined become a creative packaging idea for food on the go. These came in a white grid pattern, but you can take standard brown trays and create a grid with a white marker or draw motifs to fit the occasion. Masking tape holds down the sides. Top with napkin and fork – the fork has pieces of masking tape on the handle to add to the cuteness. Finish off with a sprig of something green on top.

3. Disposable pine wood boxes are so nice for holding food, especially these that come with a lid and are the perfect shape for fitting a sandwich or salad inside (pack in greaseproof paper). Secure with ribbon, some greenery and a name tag to make your guest feel extra special.

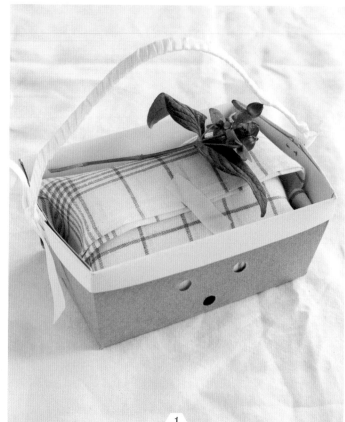

1

2

3

4

5

6

4. A baker's box in white is spruced up by adhering a strip of fabric onto the side with a glue stick, wrapping pretty ribbon around the box for colour, topping with a papier mâché mushroom from the craft shop (or anything else cute that fits your theme) and then, a wooden spoon is given new life with a strip of patterned masking tape.

5. A simple white Chinese takeaway box holds food perfectly but looks a bit more special if you place your edibles in a pretty bag, paint the edge of your natural wood fork white and glue a paper leaf to a wood stem with a ribbon to embellish. This is cute if you want to create a forest theme party that is more about the fairies than little woodland creatures (hint: girl's birthday).

6. Natural balsa wood berry baskets may be pint-sized, but if you place one on top of the other and tie tightly with a ribbon, you have enough space to fit in a wrap, some veggie sticks and a cookie. With white acrylic paint and a circular-shape sponge, make lovely dots for a modern picnic motif.

SIMPLE DIY
PATTERNED BRANCH

THIS CAN BE MADE BEFORE YOUR PARTY TO MARK THE PARTY SPOT OR LATER, DURING YOUR PARTY BY INVITING THE CHILDREN TO HELP YOU, BECAUSE IT'S EASY AND FUN. OR, FOR A PARTY YOU'RE HOSTING AT HOME, YOU CAN MAKE ONE TO DISPLAY OVER A BUFFET OR EVEN IN ANOTHER ROOM OF YOUR HOME AS ADDITIONAL DECOR.

YOU WILL NEED
a straight branch, cotton fabrics in various prints, white linen (lightweight), pine cones, thin copper wire, scissors, string

STEP ONE Tear your white linen in strips. Ours are a little over 1m/1 yard long. You could cut them neatly, but we like the torn look as it's more natural.

STEP TWO
Tie strips onto the branch. You can form a U-shape loop and lay beneath branch, then pull both ends through, or you can simply tie them on. You can also loosely wrap without tying. It's so easy, anything works!

STEP THREE Cut or tear a selection of strips from your printed fabrics.

STEP FOUR Tie the patterned strips among the white ones. Remember to keep a small space between them to insert pine cones. You can then tie string to the pine cones and tie to the branch, letting the pine cones hang at various lengths.

STEP FIVE Wrap the wire multiple times around each end of your branch, allowing enough to form a 'V' shape that you can hang from the branch of a tree.

note: You can use all creamy white linen for a different look, and use feathers instead of pine cones. Mix things up and give it a try – you'll love how it turns out.

FOREST + FAMILY

126

Playful + sweet

FUN, VIBRANT AND FILLED WITH CHARMING LITTLE DETAILS, THIS PRETTY AND AFFORDABLE LOOK IS REALLY EASY TO ACHIEVE AND YOU CAN COUNT ON HAPPY GUESTS. A GATHERING IN SWEET PASTELS IS PERFECT FOR HOSTING A SPECIAL AFTERNOON OF CUPCAKES AND CRAFTING, OR FOR CELEBRATING WITH THE YOUNGER MEMBERS OF YOUR FAMILY.

WHAT INSPIRED US... Japanese craft books; springtime flowers; favourite paper goods; watercolour paints; carnivals; and pastel sunsets. We really loved putting together this style story because we're both mums and are very active party planners. With this story, we worked hard to think of projects that could be done quickly and easily with your children (though you can use this style for a variety of occasions for grown-ups, too). This look shouldn't break the bank as we've focused mainly on paper products. Our goal is to inspire and charge up your creative engines, so have fun!

SEASON
SPRING

PARTY SUGGESTIONS
SWEET SIXTEEN
EASTER
MUM & DAUGHTER CRAFT PARTIES
MOTHER'S DAY
BIRTHDAYS
BABY SHOWER

COLOURS
MINT, PINKS, LILAC, YELLOWS
WATERCOLOUR PASTELS

PATTERNS
TINY FLORALS
BRUSH STROKES
LITTLE GEOMETRICS

ELEMENTS
SEQUINS
POM-POMS
FRUITY SWEETS
LANTERNS
GARLANDS
BALLOONS
STREAMERS
CARNATIONS
DAISIES
WASHI TAPE
BROWN WRAPPING PAPER
WATERCOLOUR PAINTS

PLAYLIST
MEGHAN TRAINOR (FEAT. JOHN LEGEND) 'LIKE I'M GONNA LOSE YOU'
SHAWN MENDES 'STITCHES'
KATY PERRY 'ROAR'
PHARRELL WILLIAMS 'HAPPY'
ONE DIRECTION 'ONE THING'

A WARM WELCOME

How could guests not love walking
into a room like this? Paper globes
are hand-painted and then hung
together with spray- painted
bunting to make the ceiling really
come alive with colour. Balloons
are blown up and scattered
around the room to play with.

These whimsical and sweet details help to create a really special CHILD'S BIRTHDAY PARTY. Carnations are arranged in ice cream cones and placed in glasses as place-setting pieces, confetti is sprinkled down the centre of the table, colourful candy kebabs top the plates and colourful straws and pretty cups make lemonade seems extra special.

TABLE RUNNER

Generic brown wrapping paper takes on a new look as a centre runner, protects the surface of your table and forms a great backdrop to all the colourful elements. Scallop the edges with scissors and outline with a white marker. Use double-sided tape to keep the runner securely in place.

EDIBLE NAPKIN RING

Stretchable candy bracelets can be used as colourful napkin rings. The soft pastel-coloured sweets are perfect for this theme.

ICE CREAM NAILS

It's fun to dress in the colours of your party and if it's for the kids, have them coordinate their outfit to the décor, too. Every detail counts so why not paint your nails in multiple colours too for a little festive fun? Small details make a big difference.

PLACE SETTINGS

Create placemats using washi tape and use white markers to write guests names on the brown paper runner. Cut round circles to place on top of the plates and then cut larger ones to place below the plates to use as chargers. Top with our candy kebabs, which are simple to make using your favourite gummies placed on a skewer, then placed on each napkin. Kids love them and for adults, they look pretty in tall drinks too!

TASTY TOPPINGS

No time to bake? Use store-bought cupcakes and make them your own by placing small non-toxic kids' toys or candies on top.

note: Not for guests under three years of age.

PLANNING TIPS FOR KIDS' PARTIES

1. Decide the appropriate duration of the party. – usually 2 to 3 hours is a good length – and how many children to invite.

2. Decide if you will host the party in your home or at an activity venue like a play centre. This works better if you want to invite a lot of kids.

3. If parents are staying, make sure to have a few snacks and drinks for them as well.

4. An itinerary helps your party run smoothly and keeps things moving, but remember to keep your timeline flexible.

5. Plan an easy activity to keep little guests busy when they are arriving and waiting for everyone to get there. It helps shy children find their feet.

6. Plan a game or two until some food is served, and then the grand finale like the cake and a piñata to end the party on a high note! All ages love a piñata!

7. Some age-appropriate games will keep the fun going. Younger ones will enjoy bubbles, dancing, freeze dance, or creating a parade to a birthday song.

8. Older children may enjoy an egg and spoon race, a scavenger hunt, pass the parcel, water balloon toss – if outside! – or a craft activity they can make and take home, such as decorate your own dessert.

9. If you plan your party time over lunchtime you will need to serve a meal of some kind. Alternatively, if you hold it in the afternoon you can just serve some drinks and snacks.

10. Keep food really simple! We find kids get so busy at parties they tend not to eat as much as you would think. Also, check for food allergies when you send out the invitation.

CONE OF FLOWERS We saw this in a favourite magazine once, only with hydrangeas, and thought to try it with the least-loved but most budget-friendly bloom out there – the carnation. With cones placed in clear glassware, you also have super-affordable vases, too.

note: Carnations can stay in cones without water for up to 8 hours before wilting.

SILK FLOWER LETTERS

DECORATE CARDBOARD LETTERS FROM THE CRAFT STORE TO CREATE WORDS. YOU CAN HANG THEM ON THE WALL ABOVE A DESSERT TABLE OR BUFFET FROM PRETTY FABRIC RIBBONS. TRY TO GET TO THE POINT – A SHORT WORD OR PHRASE WORKS BEST, SUCH AS 'LOVE', 'OH BABY', 'HAPPY DAY', 'PARTY', 'MR & MRS'. IF YOU'RE THROWING THE PARTY FOR A PARTICULAR PERSON, FOR A BIRTHDAY OR BRIDAL SHOWER, FOR INSTANCE, YOU COULD USE THE GUEST OF HONOUR'S NAME. CHOOSE FLOWERS IN COLOURS THAT BEST MIMIC NATURE TO LOOK THE MOST NATURAL. BUT IF YOU WANT TO ADD A BIT OF QUIRK, OPT FOR BLUE ROSES OR HOT PINK CARNATIONS!

YOU WILL NEED

hot glue gun, cardboard letters from the craft store, white craft paint, paint brush, ribbons, faux flowers, scissors

STEP ONE Paint your letters working from the outside in, and paint the fronts last. Two coats is best. There is no need to paint the backs.

STEP TWO When the paint is dry, flip the letters over and add your ribbon loop, with a little dab of hot glue on each side to hold it in place.

STEP THREE Lay out your flowers and remove all leaves and buds. Clip the longer ones so that all flowers are the same height when you glue them to the letter, and some aren't sticking up higher than others.

STEP FOUR Place flowers on the letters without glue and arrange using the biggest ones first, adding in a few leaves. Then grab your glue gun and apply when the arrangement looks right. If you want to keep them minimal, you can stop at this step and hang as they are.

STEP FIVE Filll the entire surface of the letters. When the glue is dry, hang on the wall above a buffet, dessert table or any open space that needs a sweet little touch.

PENNANTS

Buy ready-made generic white paper pennants (not plastic) and spray the tips lightly with spray paint – easy and gorgeous!

PAINTED LANTERNS

Plain white paper lampshade globes are so affordable and you can customize them easily using acrylic paint in painterly brush strokes. (Watercolour tends to be too wet and can damage the surface since the paper is so thin.) Arrange in a cluster from the ceiling using transparent fishing wire and a small hook.

AIR BALLOONS

No helium, no problem! To give the appearance of floating balloons blow some up, adhere to the wall with double-sided tape, curl and tie some ribbon to the bottoms, and arrange as though they're floating away. Pretty and super-budget-friendly, too!

GARLANDS

Use watercolour paints to dip the edges of cupcake cases and paper doilies in various tones. String together using a needle and strong thread and then tack to the wall.

6 ways:
PARTY HATS

1. Glue multicolour pastel sequins with craft glue to a white hat on the top and border for a little sparkle.

2. Add faux flowers to trim the hat and pop a few on top, too. A dab of glue to the base of the flower with a glue gun will keep them on just fine.

1

2

3

4

3. While that glue gun is fired up, pop on some pom-poms that you can find at any craft store or online.

4. Before you make the hat, cut out the shape and lay it flat and stamp with rubber stamps. Then create the cone-shape and add a fabric trim along the border with craft glue. Along the top of the trim, create a slim line around the entire hat using glue and sprinkle with glitter. On the top, use a paper clip to attach a paper pom-pom (you can find them pre-made in lots of stores) and a few neon ribbons.

5. Create brush strokes in a grid pattern using watercolour or acrylic paints. It's best to do this before you create the hat while it's still flat, but if you buy the hats pre-made, use a steady hand and don't worry about being perfect! Glue on some buttons as a border and pop in some feathers on top for a circus vibe.

6. Add three rows of your favourite trim along the bottom. Use a glue stick and rub it all over your hat and, over a large sheet of paper, sprinkle glitter. Using a paper punch, create a little flower. Turn up the petals a bit, glue to the hat, then glue on a little sequin centre to finish.

5

6

POPCORN BAGS

Cut pretty papers into strips to create a band. Tape together at the back. Decorate the front with washi tape and with a glue stick, add sequins. Fill with popcorn that you've mixed with candy confetti or sprinkles. These looks great assembled together in a big glass bowl on a buffet table.

sparkle + shine

THIS LOOK IS ABOUT CREATING SMALL TOUCHES TO MAKE YOUR GUESTS FEEL SPECIAL, WITH
A GLINT OF GLAMOUR: TASSELS TO ADORN A GARLAND, THE SHIMMER OF CANDLELIGHT
AND LITTLE BITS OF METALLIC CONFETTI, PRESENTS WRAPPED FOR EACH GUEST, SKEWERS FOR
SWEETS TIED WITH RIBBON. THESE TOUCHES GIVE THE PARTY A UNIQUE CHARM THAT CAN
ONLY BE CREATED WITH HEART AND A LITTLE PREPARATION.

WHAT INSPIRED US... Girlfriends who still enjoy a fancy cupcake; small presents
carefully wrapped; the shimmer of candlelight and little bits of metallic confetti; finding the
perfect pink and then having the courage to paint your dining room with it; decorating helium
balloons; gorgeous ribbons in unexpected colours; a bold and fabulous wallpaper; finding
yet another way to reuse tin cans; and knowing the magic these details can bring to an
evening with special friends.

SEASON
ANY

PARTY SUGGESTIONS
NEW YEAR'S WITH FRIENDS, SPECIAL
BIRTHDAY, DINNER WITH GIRLFRIENDS

COLOURS
PEACH, PINK, YELLOW TONES,
ORANGE, A HINT OF BLACK,
KHAKI GREEN

PATTERNS
METALLIC POLKA DOTS AND PINEAPPLES

ELEMENTS
WHITE BALLOONS
RIBBONS
GOLD SEQUINS AND CONFETTI
CORK-TOPPED TUBES
SPARKLERS
LARGE PAPER TASSELS
MIXTURE OF CANDLES AND HOLDERS
GOLD PEN
GOLD GLITTER
METALLIC PAPERS

PLAYLIST
BEBEL GILBERTO 'SO NICE'
VANESSA PARADIS 'DES QUE J'TE VOIS'
CARLA BRUNI 'QUELQU'UN M'A DIT'
COEUR DE PIRATE 'PRINTEMPS'
VANESSA DA MATA 'NAO ME DEIXE SO'
FRANCOISE HARDY 'COMMENT TE
    DIRE ADIEU'
BEBEL GILBERTO 'SAMBA DA BENCAO'
CARLA BRUNI 'LE PLUS BEAU
    DU QUARTIER'

FOILED BALLOONS

Add mini helium-filled balloons to your place settings for a more festive look. For larger balloons, tie some to the backs of chairs. You don't need to add gold foil to all balloons but using gold paper, liquid glue and a paintbrush, you can brush on glue and use your fingers to gently lay on sheets of gold paper.

PERSONAL PLACES

Place cards don't need to be typical. Try glass vials with corks and fill with confetti, sequins, glitter or anything else that you don't mind your guests throwing into the air. And of course, add their name to the vial, too.

This is AN INTIMATE ANNIVERSARY PARTY FOR A FEW CLOSE FRIENDS who mean a lot to us and whose milestone we wanted to mark. We wanted our guests to feel extra special and we decided to show them that with warm metallic details and lots of sweet homemade charm. Then, after dinner, we turned up the music and celebrated!

SWEET SKEWERS

Marshmallows are dipped in chocolate, rolled in nuts and then skewered individually with a plain marshmallow. These make for a fun sweet treat to serve, especially when tied with some pretty bows!

QUILT WRAPPING

Bits of paper are quilted together with washi tape to create wrapping paper for these small boxes of chocolates. Each guest gets to enjoy this sweet surprise!

WASHI CAKE STAND

Cupcakes look extra special when you place them on a white cake stand that has been decorated with just a few pieces of gold washi tape and a couple of circles cut from thick metallic paper.

SOFT DRINKS

If you have a cocktail party, always make sure to include non-alcoholic beverages for those guests not imbibing. In glass bottles, we've added store-bought lemonades, spritzers and juices and labelled each with a pretty handwritten tag.

SPARKLERS

Don't save sparklers for just the children's parties! Pop them in some special little cakes to make your dessert course feel extra festive. They burn very quickly so light them for your guests to enjoy immediately!

PLAYFUL SETTING

Have fun with your knives and forks!
Try casually tying them with a bit of pretty
wired ribbon to create an interesting,
playful place setting.

anna cecile

TIN CAN LANTERNS

DIY PROJECTS DO NOT HAVE TO BE DIFFICULT TO ADD THAT EXTRA SPECIAL ELEMENT TO YOUR NEXT PARTY. GET SOME SPARKLE IN YOUR HALLWAY OR SOME TWINKLE ON YOUR MANTEL WITH THESE SIMPLE TIN CAN LANTERNS. MAKE SURE TO MAKE AT LEAST SIX OF THESE TO GET THE LOOK, THE MORE THE MERRIER!

YOU WILL NEED

cleaned tin cans, spray paint, nails in various sizes, light gauge metal wire, hammer, decorative tapes, large sequins or glitter, glue, tealights.

STEP ONE Spray paint the cans outside in a well-ventilated area. Alternatively, you can paint the outside of the cans using a brush and a non-toxic acrylic paint.

STEP TWO Using different-sized nails (of various diameters), carefully hammer holes into the cans. We like to focus the holes near the bottom of the cans where the candlelight can glow through.

STEP THREE Once you have made all your desired holes, decorate your cans with some metallic tapes and glue on some sequins for extra sparkle!

STEP FOUR It is also nice to attach a handle to a can or two so that you could hang your lantern if desired. Create two holes near the top of your can on opposite sides and thread your wire through to create a handle.

6 ways:
WHITE
BALLOONS

1. Turn generic white balloons into the life of the party with a few craft supplies and about 5 minutes or less per balloon. For a glittery look brush on some craft glue using a foam applicator and then sprinkle with large glitter while still wet. Allow to dry. These designs are all light enough to float when filled with helium. Alternatively, you can stick balloons to the wall using tape or let them lay on the floor or tabletop.

2. Brush on 3 different colours of acrylic craft paint in simple sweeping brush strokes to create this painterly effect. Allow to dry – this usually takes less than 30 minutes.

3. Large packs of star stickers are sold at teacher supply shops and they look sweet on balloons. They are inexpensive and one pack can go a long way!

4. Basic round office supply sheets of stickers are painted with one colour, allowed to dry and then peeled and applied to the balloon. This is a nice way to get clean, custom-colour polka dots on your balloons.

5. Gold acrylic craft paint is brushed onto the bottom third of the balloon and allowed to dry.

6. Use a gold craft pen to write on a balloon. The possibilities here are endless. We have even seen a dinner party menu written on a large white balloon!

CONVERSATION STARTER

Tie beautiful fabric ribbons to balloons
in the palette of your party and on each
balloon create a little name tag so that
guests are invited to find the balloon with
their name on it. This is a fun little way to
invite interaction among guests.

MUST-SHOP SOURCES

UNITED KINGDOM

PARTY SUPPLIES

Cass Art
cassart.co.uk

Julie Rose Party Co.
julierosepartyco.co.uk

Peach Blossom
peachblossom.co.uk

Ginger Ray
gingerray.co.uk

Hobbycraft
hobbycraft.co.uk

V. V. Rouleaux
vvrouleaux.com

Fred Aldous
fredaldous.co.uk

Paper Mash
papermash.co.uk

Pearl & Earl
pearlandearl.com

Chilpa
etsy.com/shop/WeAreChilpa

Paper Ten
etsy.com/shop/PaperTen

TABLEWARE

Anthropologie
anthropologie.co.uk

Butlers
butlers-online.co.uk

Dinosaur Designs
dinosaurdesigns.co.uk

Jonathan Adler
uk.jonathanadler.com

Liberty
liberty.co.uk

Selfridges
selfridges.co.uk

West Elm
westelm.co.uk

UNITED STATES & CANADA

PARTY SUPPLIES

Sweet Lulu
shopsweetlulu.com

Ban.do
shopbando.com

Eco Party Time
ecopartytime.com

Meri Meri
merimeri.com

The Flair Exchange
shop.theflairexchange.com

Martha Stewart Crafts
marthastewartcrafts.com

Michaels
michaels.com

Paper Source
papersource.com

Oh Happy Day Shop
shop.ohhappyday.com

Zazzle
zazzle.com

Minted
minted.com

TABLEWARE

The Cross Design
thecrossdesign.com

ABC Carpet & Home
abchome.com

Anthropologie
anthropologie.com

Huset
huset-shop.com

General Store
shop-generalstore.com

Heather Taylor Home
heathertaylorhome.com

Pottery Barn
potterybarn.com

Jonathan Adler
jonathanadler.com

West Elm
westelm.com

Sarah Sherman Samuel
sarahshermansamual.com

Lulu and Georgia
luluandgeorgia.com

Pigeonhole Home Store
pigeonholehomestore.com

EUROPE

PARTY SUPPLIES

Blue Box Tree
blueboxtree.com

Idee
idee-shop.com

Der Papierladen Mesecke
facebook.com/Papierladen.
Hannover

Partyerie
partyerie.de

La Mesa
lamesa.de

HEMA
hema-deutschland.de

RICE
Rice.dk

PomPom Manufaktur
pompom- manufaktur.de

Rico Design
rico-design.de

MT Masking Tape
mt-maskingtape.com

TABLEWARE

Butlers
butlers.de

Anthropologie
anthropologie.de

Bloomingville
bloomingville.com

Westwing Now
westwingnow.de

Indigo Blumenladen
indigoblumen.de

Depot
depot-online.com

Dishes Only
dishesonly.com

Kukkamari
kukkamari.de

Merci
merci-merci.com

AUSTRALIA

PARTY SUPPLIES

Eckersley's
eckersleys.com.au

Emiko Blue
emikoblue.com

Confetti & Cake
confettiandcake.com.au

Poppies For Grace
poppiesforgrace.com

Ready To Party
readytoparty.com.au

Favor Lane
favorlane.com.au

Miss Bunting
missbunting.com

Sucre Shop
sucreshop.com

My Messy Room
mymessyroom.com.au

Pink Frosting
pinkfrosting.com.au

The Party Provider
thepartyprovider.com.au

Simply Sweet Soirees
simplysweetsoirees.com.au

TABLEWARE

From The Owl
fromtheowl.com

Donna Hay
donnahay.com.au

Dinosaur Designs
dinosaurdesigns.com.au

Elephant Ceramics
elephantceramics.com

Mud Australia
mudaustralia.com

West Elm
westelm.com.au

Wheel & Barrow
wheelandbarrow.com.au

VERY SPECIAL THANKS

A special thanks to Jacqui Small and team for giving me the wings to produce work that makes me happy. To our book designer Helen Bratby, thank you for your endless support, boundless energy and overall dedication to this project. Extra thanks to our super fab editor Sian Parkhouse for being so good at what you do. It's always such a pleasure to work with you.

Thank you Jessy Senti for being the best assistant ever and to my contributing writers on decor8 and others who help me with my business, especially when I'm writing books and my life gets chaotic. I appreciate your dedication and support.

To the additional photographers who made this book so lovely: Laure Joliet, Holly Marder, Janis Nicolay with special photos from Kelly Brown and Anouschka Rokebrand. Thank you for your energy, great eye and talent. Thank you to our many friends and family who helped us on shoots and to our models and the homeowners who so generously let us create in your beautiful homes.

To Esra Celik, Tinna Pedersen, Angela Brabänder, Sania Pell and Kristina Schurzig for always listening, caring and for being great friends. Thank you Toni Vinther for being a constant source of light, laughter and friendship (and for Paris).

Thank you to my dear friends Leslie and Dan. I have such deep gratitude and respect for you both. I have learned so much from you and can't wait to celebrate the launch of this book with you again in London and abroad.

Thank you Aidan, my little boy, because your smiles, kisses and giggles encourage and inspire me so much. You may be too small to understand now, but when you read this some day please know that having you in my life has brought more sunshine than I ever hoped for and has given me the energy I need to stay on track. You are my greatest muse. I loved having you with me on some of the photo shoots in this book and how happy you were to touch and play with everything as much as we were. I couldn't have custom-ordered a better boy. My wish is to lead by example with nothing but love and be a good role model for you. I love you boopy.

Thank you to my husband Thorsten and to my dear friends and fans of decor8 – I never want to forget my roots and to show my gratitude for all you've done to support my work. *Holly*

Thank you Jacqui Small for another opportunity to work on a creative project that I really love. You have a brilliant team who help make this all happen. Our patient editor Sian Parkhouse is truly the best; I feel lucky to work with her again. Our talented book designer Helen Bratby – an honour to work with you again, you really bring this project to life in a beautiful way.

Big thank you to photographers Laure Joliet and Holly Marder – your work is inspiring, it was a pleasure to work with you and you both have helped make this project more gorgeous. A special thank you to my friend and photographer Janis Nicolay; I feel absolutely fortunate to work with you again. You are pure gold.

Big thanks to our lovely models and very generous homeowners for making the shoots possible.

A special thank you to styling assistant Cindy Lin, calligrapher Kate Campbell and my friend Julie Cove for all your help.

Thank you to Holly Becker for being my partner in creativity.

Thank you to all my family who always help me and who have to deal with me through these projects. Caitlin, you are such a blessing, this book would not be the same without all your help. Diane, thank you for being a good sport and doing so much. Thank you to Sienna and Parker for all your understanding of your busy mommy.

And finally to Dan: thank you, thank you, thank you. *Leslie*

CONTRIBUTORS

CANADA
Locations
Julie Cove, alkalinesisters.com
Pam Lewis and Metka
Lazar of Moonrise Creative,
moonrisecreative.ca

Styling assistants
Diane Shewring
Caitlin Sheehan, instagram.com/
caitlinls
Josh Larsen, instagram.com/
joshualars
Divine Bartolome

Calligraphy
Kate Campbell, instagram.com/
kateandcampbell11

Flowers
Thorn & Thistle, thornandthistle.ca

Props
Bash Specialty, bashspecialty.com
Shop Sweet Lulu, shopsweetlulu.com
Pigeonhole Home Store,
pigeonholehomestore.com

LOS ANGELES
Locations
Sarah Sherman Samuel and Rupert
Samuel, sarahshermansamuel.com
Heather Taylor,
heathertaylorhome.com

Styling assistants
Cindy Lin, staged4more.com

Flowers
Silver Lake Farms,
silverlakefarms.com

GERMANY
Locations
Anette Wetzel-Grolle, lebenslustiger.
com
Eilenriede Forest Hannover,
hannover.de
Lister Turm Biergarten, lister-turm-
biergarten-hannover.de

Styling assistants
Susanne Irmer, milas-deli.com
Pamuk Akkaya, instagram.com/
pamukak

Flowers
Indigo, indigoblumen.de

Props
RICE, rice.dk
PomPom Manufaktur, pompom-
manufaktur.de
Shop Sweet Lulu, shopsweetlulu.com
ComingHome Interiors,
cominghome-interior.de
Superfront, superfront.com
Bloomingville, bloomingville.com
Connox, connox.de
La Mesa, lamesa.de
Mooi Moin, Rambergstr 32,
Hannover, Germany
Kukkamari, kukkamari.de
Muuto, muuto.com
Niner Bakes, ninerbakes.com
Fashion For Home,
fashionforhome.de
Aimée Wilder, aimeewilder.com
Dear Lilly, Sedanstr. 37, Hannover,
Germany
Farrow & Ball, farrow-ball.com
Agentur Pedersen,
agenturpedersen.com
Dishes Only, dishesonly.com

Anna Westerlund,
annawesterlund.com
West Elm, westelm.com
Zazzle, zazzle.com
Minted, minted.com

THE NETHERLANDS
Locations
Holly Marder, avenuelifestyle.com

Props
Sukha, sukha-amsterdam.nl

MODELS
**A special thank you to our lovely
friends and family who appear in
this book:**
Sienna Sheehan, p. 132, 135
Aidan Benjamin Becker, p. 120,
122
Caitlin Sheehan, instagram.com/
caitlinls p. 9, 36 top left, 39, 49,
54, 103, 106, 109
Josh Larsen, instagram.com/
joshualars, p. 106
Holly Marder, avenuelifestyle.com
p. 1, 20, 25, 62, 153
Esra Celik, p. 90, 91, 95
Sean Andrew Shackelford, p. 90
Sarah Sherman Samuel,
sarahshermansamuel.com, p.14,
50, 54
Pamuk Akkaya, instagram.com/
pamukak, p. 21, 25, 31 top right
and bottom left
Lilly Oppitz, p. 4, 90, 95
Tinna Pedersen, agenturpedersen.
com, p. 25
Emma Pedersen, p. 90, 95, 101
Carey Salvdor,
pigeonholehomestore.com, p.6
Cara Triconi p.6
Agata Atmore,
islandgeneralshoppe.com, p.6
Metka Lazar, moonrisecreative.ca,
p.39
Pam Lewis, moonrisecreative.ca,
p.39

PHOTOGRAPHY
CREDITS

LESLIE SHEWRING
leslieshewring.com
page 20 bottom, far right, 26 (all), 27, 29, 33, 34 (all), 35, 44 (all), 45, 48 (all), 50 top, middle right, 51 top, 56 right, 57 top, 58 (all), 59, 60 (all), 62 (all except middle right), 63 top, 68 right, 69 left, 72 (all), 73, 74 top left, middle, 75 top, 81, 87 (all), 102 middle right, bottom, 103 (all), 105, 106 (all), 107, 108 (all), 109, 110, 111 (all), 112 (all), 113, 119 top right, 120 right, 128 top left, bottom, 129 bottom, 131, 132 top left, top right, bottom right, 133, 135, 138 (all), 139 (all), 140 top left, top right, middle left, 142 (all except middle right), 145, 146, 147 top right, bottom left, bottom right, 148, 149, 150 (all), 151,152 (all).

HOLLY BECKER
decor8blog.com
page 1, 2, 3, 4, 13, 16, 20 top, left, middle, 21 top, 22, 24 top right, 25, 30, 31 top left, top right, bottom right, 32, 38, 50 left, 52, 61, 64, 70 (all), 71 (all), 75 bottom, 76, 85, 88 (all), 89, 90 (all), 91 (all), 92, 93, 94, 95 (all), 96, 97, 98, 99 (all), 100 (all), 101, 104, 114 (all except top and far right), 115 (all), 116, 120 left, 121 (all), 122 (all), 123, 124 (all), 125 (all), 126 (all), 127, 128 top right, middle left, middle right, 129 top right, 130, 132 bottom left, 134, 136 (all), 137, 140 middle right, bottom left, bottom right, 141, 142 middle right, 144, 153, 160.

HOLLY MARDER
avenuelifestyle.com
page 10, 17, 20 bottom, 21 bottom, 23, 24 top left, bottom left, bottom right, 28, 31 bottom left, 36 middle left, middle right, bottom, 37 top, 62 middle right, 63 bottom, 65, 66/67, 68 left, 69 right, 117, 118, 119 top left, bottom left, bottom right, 143 (all), 147 top left, 157.

LAURE JOLIET
laurejoliet.com
page14, 15, 50 bottom, far right, 51 bottom, 53, 54 (all), 55, 56 top left, 57 bottom, 102 top left, middle left, middle centre.

KELLY BROWN
kellybrownphotographer.com
page 18/19.

JANIS NICOLAY
janisnicolay.com
page 6, 9, 36 top left, middle, 37 bottom, 39, 40/41, 42 (all), 43, 46, 47 (all), 49, 74 middle left, middle right, bottom, 77, 78 (all), 79, 80, 82 (all), 83 (all), 84, 86.

ANOUSCHKA ROKEBRAND
anouschkarokebrand.com
page 114 top, far right, Holly Becker author's photo on back of jacket.

SUSANNE IRMER
milas-deli.com
page 148

Our wish is that this book has inspired and encouraged you to celebrate more often but with less stress, to create pretty things by hand and, when decorating for a party, to strive for heartfelt versus perfection. Let's all focus more on what matters most – not overwhelming your guests but making them feel happy, accepted and loved, and helping them walk away inspired to create beautiful parties of their own. Xo